TABLE OF CONTENTS

ILLUSTRATIONS

CHAPTER ONE

INTRODUCTION

"In complex war, we will encounter adversaries who possess greater lethality than postulated in recent conceptual thinking. This diffusion of lethality, especially to non-state entities, means that the apparent benign missions can rapidly escalate into intense combat. Army force elements need to be able to survive initial contact with these adversaries and be able to deliver decisive and lethal force in response to their fire. Sustained close combat remains the Army's core task and its unique contribution to the Government's range of military options". Lieutenant General Peter Leahy, AO, 29 August 2003.[1]

Background

The tragic effects of September 2001 and the Bali Bombings of October 2002 sent clear shock waves to both the Australian Government and the Australian people. These shock waves have resulted in realignment of the priorities that drive Australian foreign policy, national interest and priorities for defense. For the Australian Army this is an important change, as shackles that previously restricted Army have been broken. The strategic guidance that provides this new direction for a modernized Australian Army is published in two key documents: *Australia's National Security: A Defence Update* 2003 and the *Defence Capability Plan 2003* (DCP).[2] These documents indicate a paradigm shift in Australian defense policy from the traditional 'defense of Australia' (DOA) doctrine to the dialectic between Australia's geographic and global interests.

Defense guidance highlights that the future will contain a perplexing, complex array of security challenges for Australia. The effects of globalization, the Global War on Terror

---

[1] This statement was made in a short paper addressed to all Army start rank officers informing the Australian Army senior leadership why the Chief of Army believed that Army must change. See: Leahy Peter, LTGEN, Chief of the Australian Army, Minute OCA/OUT/2003/1457, *Hardening the Army*, dated 29 August 2003.

[2] One key change articulated for Army in these documents is the decision to upgrade the current in-service tank. While the decision has been made to procure replacement tanks, no decision has been made on the type of tank. Two choices seem to exist: the German design Leopard II or the US M1A1 Abrams. See Ian McPhedran "Hill in talks to buy Leopards, *The Herald Sun.* 09 January 2004, [On-line]; available from http://www heraldsun news.com.au/common/story_page/0,5478,8360908%255E662,00.html This article suggests that the Leopard II may be the tank of choice due to cost effectiveness. Discussion on

(GWOT), and the post Cold War climate have created the need for militaries worldwide to review their force structure, capabilities and doctrine. Like the US, the Australian Army is examining its structure. While past DOA doctrine placed emphasis on Sea and Air priorities, it occurred at a cost to Army. This impacted on Army's ability to present the Australian Government with acceptable land force options for deployment to Iraq (OIF) or Afghanistan (OEF).[3] This limitation is under review.

The Chief of the Australian Army (CA) Lieutenant General Peter Leahy's response to the challenges of the global and complex environment and needs of Government is what he terms 'hardening the Army'.[4] He argues that Army must have enhanced force protection, firepower, and agility and be more closely integrated into Joint and Coalition frameworks. Using observations from operations in Afghanistan, Iraq, and East Timor, the CA states: "Army must move from a light infantry force to a light armored force with increased protection, firepower and mobility. The alternative is for us to steadily lose capability over time as existing systems age and are overwhelmed by the emerging threat environment."[5] The hardened force must become mobile, agile, flexible and versatile or risk being incapable of serving Australia's vital interests.[6]

The Australian Army Future Land Warfare (FLW) Directorate has submitted a proposal to Government to support the CA's hardening initiative. In essence this proposal recommends force structure changes to modernize the Australian Army. It is the intent of this research paper to generate further discussion of this topic, through an examination of Australian strategic

---

the type of tank and even the need of a new tank remains a topic of debate within Australian Defence circles. A final decision on the replacement tank is expected in early 2004.

[3] ADF force package deployments to OIF and OEF were based on a Special Air Service Squadron, with supporting arms, CSS and aviation assets

[4] Lieutenant General Peter Leahy, AO, Address to the Land Warfare Conference, 28 October 2003, [On-line]; available from www.defence.gov.au/army. In this speech Lieutenant General Leahy, states that Army's response to the challenges posed by Complex War Fighting and Government guidance, must be met by a 'harder Army'. As such, he has directed within Army a process called 'hardening'. He sees this process as being critical for future Army success on the future battlefield.

[5] Lieutenant General Peter Leahy, AO, Address to the United Service Institution of the Australian Capital Territory, Australia , 11 June 2003, [On-line]; available www.defence.gov.au/army.

guidance, the perceived nature of future warfare, the proposed FLW hardened solution and an overall analysis. Insights and exposure to the US transformation concept will assist in this research.

Problem statement

Will the hardening process support the needs of the Australian Government, within the constraints of the Australian Defense budget, while addressing the future threat-ambiguous strategic environment of warfare? If so, do conditions demand force structure initiatives for a more flexible, balanced and adaptive Australian Army? As expressed by one defense analyst "Defense and Alliance officials are now faced with the difficult problem of translating the implications of a threat-ambiguous strategic environment into defense planning and force development methodologies that are applicable to modern military structures and convincing cost conscious politicians."[7]

Many elements within Defence are still caught up in the dialectic regarding what should drive the future structure of the Australian Army? Is the answer: home defense; options for Government to deploy land forces to fight in foreign conflict; or purely a focus on counter-terrorist capabilities? As stated by the CA, "the idea that Australia can choose between such options is wrong."[8] The truth is that Australia must structure for all three requirements.[9]

---

[6] Peter Leahy "A Land Force for the Future: The Australian Army in the Early 21ˢᵗ Century." *Australian Army Journal,* vol. 1 (June 2003): 27.

[7] Thomas-Durell Young, "Capabilities-Based Defense Planning: The Australian Experience" *Armed Forces and Society*, vol. 21, no. 3, (Spring 1995): 349.

[8] Leahy "A Land Force for the Future: The Australian Army in the Early 21ˢᵗ Century." 19.

[9] Doctrinally these options are now reflected as campaign options for government as part of the complex warfighting environment, whether conducted within Australian territory or offshore. These components are titled as MOLE, PSAT and CCOW. PSAT = Protective security operations on Australian territory provide a secure, firm base area for all military campaigns. PSAT activities will always occur, during any type of campaign. MOLE = Maneuver Operations in the Littoral Environment. CCOW. Contributions to Coalition Operations Worldwide represent the most diverse form of land force campaign. For further details regarding campaign concepts see: Australia Department of Defence. *Complex Warfighting* (Draft version 3.2). Canberra, Australia: Future Land Warfare Branch, Oct 2003: Annex B-3.

To harden the Australian Army, requires an ability to rethink strategic imperatives and adjust from traditional mindsets. While many recent lessons may be available from experiences in East Timor, the Solomon Islands, Afghanistan and Iraq, one must be cautious that such experiences do not bias proposed capability and force structure. It is the intent of this paper to examine the hardening concept, the proposals presented by FLW and, if appropriate, present an alternative option for consideration.

Methodology

The first portion of the study and research will begin by defining why the Australian Army must change. This will be a needs analysis comparing the needs of the Australian Government with the capabilities of the Australian Army. Government needs will be based on Australia's national interests (both global and regional), recent strategic guidance, influences, and the Australian Army definition of the nature of future warfare. Key references for this research include: "The Fundamentals of Land Warfare 2002;" Australia's National Security: "A Defence Update 2003; The Australian Defence Force 2020; and the Australian Army, "Future Warfighting Concept (DRAFT) Oct 2003."

The second portion of this study and research will detail the "hardening" concept and proposed FLW force structure. The FLW proposal will be examined to identify strengths and / or expose limitations. This will be achieved by conducting a comparative analysis of Australia's needs with the 'hardening concept'.

The final portion of this study will conclude by discussing the effectiveness of the identified hardening force structure proposal, highlighting limitations, and if appropriate, recommending an alternative force structure option.

Assumptions

This monograph assumes that the future battlefield environment detailed in the Department of Defence *"Future Warfighting Concept"* as the doctrinal environment basis for this study. It also assumes that no significant change will occur to the current Australian Defence budget (1.9% of GDP) or imposed manpower ceiling.

Limitations

The focus of this monograph is solely on the transformation of the Australian Army. No attempt is made to examine the second or third order effects that a change in Army structure may have for the Royal Australian Navy or the Royal Australian Air Force. The hardening concept also addresses cost effective geographical aspects of force structure that is outside the scope of this study.

Method of Evaluation

Three key source documents have been selected as the basis of evaluation. These are: the Australian Army, Land Warfare Doctrine 1 (LWD 1): *The Fundamentals of Land Warfare,* Future Land Warfare Branch (Australian Army) *Complex Warfighting* (Draft version 3.2); and Huba Wass de Czege and Richard Hart Sinnreich, *Conceptual Foundations of a Transformed US Army.* These documents have been selected because they collectively cover the spectrum of Australian doctrine, the future threat-ambiguous strategic environment and theory. Four derived evaluation terms, employed in this paper are 'balance and adaptability' and 'flexibility and modularity'. Details regarding the selected method of evaluation, an explanation of the four terms and supporting notes is detailed in Appendix A.

CHAPTER TWO

AUSTRALIA'S NATIONAL INTERESTS, DEFENCE POLICY AND ALLIANCES

Australia's interests are global in scope and not solely defined by geography' Department of Foreign Affairs and Trade White Paper, *Advancing the National Interest*, 2003

"The horrific Bali bombings last year and the threat of the proliferation of weapons of mass destruction in Iraq and North Korea remind us that we cannot take our security for granted. And economic globalisation will continue to test Australia and our partners in the region and beyond.... It reinforces the Government's strong commitment to strengthening our key relationships wherever these are in the world, as Australia's interests become increasingly global."[10]

The 2003 White Paper, "Advancing the Nations Interests" details three categories that describe Australia's National interests: the maintenance of security and prosperity, the consolidation and expansion of Australia's bilateral and regional relationships, and the protection of Australia and its values. It is important to acknowledge that the document reflects Australian interests that are global in scope and not solely defined by geography. This reflection is a result of the defining terrorist events of 11 September 2001 in the United States and the 12 October 2002 Bali Bombing. These events have shaped Australia's security environment in a significant way demonstrating that threats to Australia's security are both global and regional. This combined global interest in turn influences Australian strategic defense policy and the posture of the Australian Defence Force (ADF). [11]

Australia maintains the ADF for one primary reason: warfighting, defined as the application of organized force in combat. Australia's armed forces are placed in harms way for one essential reason, the pursuit of Australia's national interests. Warfighting is therefore the

---

[10] Joint Media Release, Senator Alexander Downer The Minister for Foreign Affairs,and the Minister for Trade, 12 February 2003 Advancing the National Interest [Online] available from http://www foreignminister.gov.au/releases/2003/fa010b_03 html

ADF's unique contribution to national security.[12] Since WW II, this unique contribution has been shaped by influences ranging from an emphasis on the "defense of Australia (DOA)",[13] the alliance with the United States (ANZUS Treaty)[14], an emphasis on self-reliance, Government interest in international peacekeeping, regional stability, through to the lasting impacts of the Vietnam War. In one or more ways these factors have shaped Australian Defense policy.

Australia's involvement in the Vietnam War demonstrated that it could not make an open-ended commitment to a US-led coalition, particularly for land operations, without clearly defined reasons for involvement and clearly identified end-states. The Australian Government could not afford to suffer high Australian casualties without an unambiguous national understanding of the underlying reasons for involvement.[15]

Within Defence circles much debate exists regarding Australia's strategic guidance, the pursuit of national interests and the design of the ADF's force structure.[16] Within the current Government, contrasting perspectives exist. Recently the Defence Minister, Senator Robert Hill stated that the capability to safely deploy, lodge and sustain Australian forces offshore is of vital

---

[11] Australian Department of Foreign Affairs and Trade. *Australian Foreign and Trade Policy White Paper: Advancing the National Interests*, Canberra, Australia: National Capital Printing 2003: iv-xiii, 6-8.
[12] Australian Department of Defence. *Future Warfighting Concept.* Canberra, Australia: National Capital printing, 2003: 5.
[13] Defense of Australia, otherwise known as DOA, is premised on the structure of the ADF towards homeland defense. For further details, see Jeffrey Grey. *A Military History of Australia.* Melbourne, Australia, Cambridge University Press, 1990: 247-256.
[14] Australia's ANZUS alliance with the United States is fundamental to national security. The ANZUS commitment to consult and act against a common threat is directly relevant to the defense of Australia and of US engagement in Asia. Strengthened by fifty years of cooperation, ANZUS continues to be the foundation of a dynamic and broad-ranging security relationship, which includes joint exercises, exchange personnel, the sharing of strategic assessments and the exchange of intelligence. IT is important to also highlight that the ANZUS treaty also includes New Zealand. See: Australian Department of Foreign Affairs and Trade. *Australian Foreign and Trade Policy White Paper: Advancing the National Interests*, Canberra, Australia: National Capital Printing 2003: 88.
[15] Alan Ryan. *Australian Army Cooperation with the Land Forces of the United States, Problems of the Junior Partner.* Duntroon, Canberra, Australia: Study Paper no. 121, Land Warfare Studies Centre, 2002: 16.
[16] The basis to such conflicting perspectives is the aforementioned influences on the various sectors of government, military and defense theorists, ranging from the Vietnam War through to the rigid belief that the military should only been structured purely for homeland defense. Recent defense articles even question whether a realistic capability exists today to actually invade Australia.

importance to the Government. In the same article, the Australian Prime Minister stated that Government believes that DOA doctrine is the primary driver for future ADF force structure.[17] These comments cause confusion.

Updated strategic guidance[18] combined with diverse perspectives causes further confusion. The recent $50 billion Defence capability plan is viewed by some as the end of the DOA doctrine that has driven Australian national defense policy for 25 years.[19] This doctrine is viewed by others as having seriously eroded core land force capabilities and turned the Army into little more than a strategic goalkeeper.[20]

Four key defense policy documents outline the changing view of defense priorities in response to the rapidly changing strategic environment: *1997 Australian Strategic Policy; Defence 2000, Defence Update 2003 and the Defence Capability Review.* These four key policy papers will be examined.

1997 Australian Strategic Policy

The 1997 Australian Strategic Policy began the course for developing a more flexible, capable, balanced, ready and sustainable Australian military, focused on protecting Australia and its national interests. It changed the previous emphasis from low level operations to developing the right level and mix of capabilities necessary for defense self-reliance.[21] The policy stressed the capacity to defend Australia in a wide range of circumstances by focusing on the maritime

---

[17] Patrick Walters, "50BN for New Defence Arsenal" *The Australian* (Canberra) 08 November 2003 [Online] available from http://www.theaustralian news.com.au/

[18] The Australian Government released two new documents: Defence Update 2003 and the Defence Capability Review in November 2003 as updated strategic guidance.

[19] Ian Mcphedran, "Tanks to Lead Defence of the Future" *Courier Mail* (Brisbane) 08 November 2003 , [Online]; available from http://www.thecouriermail news.com.au /

[20] Peter Leahy "A Land Force for the Future: The Australian Army in the Early 21st Century." (June 2003): 23.

[21] Australia's 1997 Defence Policy Statement [On-Line]; available from http://www.dfat.gov.au/arf/documents/1997defp.pdf

approaches. The policy also initiated a clear inextricable link between Australia's security and the

security of the region"[22]

Defence 2000

The Capability Goal highlight of Defence 2000 was "The Government's aim is to provide land forces that can respond swiftly and effectively to any credible armed lodgment on Australian territory and provide forces for more likely types of operations in our immediate neighborhood. We have therefore decided that it is no longer a priority to provide the basis for the rapid expansion of the Army to a size required for major continental-scale operations. Rather, we place emphasis on providing a professional, well-trained, well-equipped force that is available for operations at short notice, and one that can be sustained over extended periods. This type of force will have the flexibility to deal with operations other than conventional war, and contribute to coalitions."[23]

Defence 2000 is premised on the belief that Australia's strategic policy is to prevent any

credible armed attack on Australia.[24] Defence 2000 detailed five strategic interests and objectives:

1. Ensure the defense of Australia and its direct approaches;
2. Foster the security of Australia's immediate neighborhood;
3. Promote stability and cooperation in Southeast Asia;
4. Support strategic stability in the wider Asia Pacific Region; and
5. Support global security.[25]

To provide Government with the flexibility to deal with the complexity of warfare,

Defence 2000 directed Army to be structured and resourced to be able to sustain a brigade on

operations while maintaining at least a battalion group available for deployment elsewhere.[26] To

achieve this intent, force structure was to be based on six regular infantry battalions groups.[27]

This guidance is at best ambiguous, because only five conventional infantry battalions exist.[28]

---

[22] The Hon Ian McLachlan, Minister for Defence, Address to the House of Representatives, 02 December 1997, [Online] ; available from http://www.defence.gov.au/minister/sr97/s971202.html

[23] Australian Department of Defence, *Defence 2000.* Canberra, Australia: Australian Government Publishing Service, 2000: 78-79.

[24] Ibid., 29.

[25] Ibid., 30-31.

[26] Ibid., XIII-XIV.

[27] Ibid., 2000: 80.

[28] Ibid.,   While highlighting the need for a six infantry battalion capability, Defence 2000 directs that the commando battalion is part of Special Forces command and as such is assigned unique special forces related tasks. The total available high readiness infantry battalions are therefore reduced from six to five. For further example on the implications Army has in both sustaining and rotating its land combat forces within the realistic five battalion structure See: Alan Ryan. *Australian Army Cooperation with the*

The concept / requirement / tenet of operational flexibility is a recurring theme in Defence 2000.[29] The provision of one set of capabilities must be flexible enough to provide Government with a range of military options across a spectrum of credible situations, using the military in circumstances that may not have previously been envisioned.[30] Defense planning and force structure initiatives cannot afford to shape the Army with a set of capabilities that is too narrow. Force structure must be flexible and deployable, an issue that will be discussed when examining the hardening process.[31]

Defence Update 2003

The Defence Review 2003 highlights the changing security environment: the emergence of new and immediate threats from terrorism and the increased concerns about the proliferation of weapons of mass destruction. The document states that while the principles set out in the Defence White Paper 2000 remain sound, changes in Australia's strategic environment have caused the

---

Land Forces of the United States, Problems of the Junior Partner. Study Paper no. 121, Land Warfare Studies Centre, Duntroon, Canberra, Australia, 2002: 11.

[29] One example of this reoccurring theme is a statement by the then Minister of Defence, Peter Reith. When Defence 2000 was released, Minister Reith stated: "the aim is to provide Australia with a set of capabilities that will be flexible enough to provide governments with a range of military options across a spectrum of credible situations and give the ADF the capability to play a positive role in promoting and supporting stability and cooperation in the region." See: address by Defence Minister Peter Reith, "Ministers Message." *Australian Defence Force Journal,* vol 147 (Marl/Apr 2001): 3.

[30] Australian Department of Defence. *Future Warfighting Concept,* 54.

[31] A Bergin. "Steady As-You-Go." Australian Defence Force Journal .No 147 (Mar/Apr 2001): 21-22

necessity to rebalance capability and expenditure.[32] Factors such as less strategic certainty require

flexibility and adaptability to answer the unexpected as much as the expected.[33]

Hugh White, the principal author of 'Defence 2000', presents another perspective. [34]

White writes

> "If we will have fewer but bigger tanks, fewer but bigger ships, fewer strike
> aircraft, fewer airborne early warning aircraft, and fewer, much bigger
> amphibious troop transport ships. Is Australia increasing her capability to handle
> lower-intensity unconventional operations, or higher-intensity conventional
> conflicts? The review was supposed to reshape the Australian Defence Force to
> respond to the kinds of security threats since September 11, 2001. Conventional
> wisdom says these new threats come more from terrorists, transnational criminals
> and insurgents than from traditional military adversaries."[35]

White's comments reflect further confusion and misunderstanding within Defence, highlighting

the need for a clear and unambiguous purpose of the hardening concept.

Defence Capability Review 2003

> Australian Defence Minister, Senator Robert Hill stated "after reviewing our
> defense capabilities, the Government has decided to provide the ADF with new
> assets, equipment and capabilities that will ensure it continues to be able to
> defend Australia and Australian interests in an uncertain and complex
> environment,"[36]

---

[32] *Australia's National Security: A Defence Update 2003*, (Canberra, Australia: Australian Government Publishing Service, 2003), 6. A key example of change from past guidance is: Defence 2000 stated that government decided against the development of heavy armored forces suitable for contributions to coalition forces in high intensity conflicts, because such forces are expensive, and are not within the bounds of National interests. See Australian Department of Defence, *Defence 2000.* Canberra, Australia: Australian Government Publishing Service, 2000: 79. This policy belief was also highlighted in the previous 1997 Strategic Policy Paper. See Paul Dibb. "The Relevance of the Knowledge Edge." *Australian Defence Force Journal,* vol 134 (Jan/Feb 1999): 39. Dibb states "that Australia did not need to excel in heavy armored warfare as it does not expect to operate in that environment, either in the north of Australia or overseas" This guidance changed with Defence Update 2003.

[33] *Australia's National Security: A Defence Update 2003,* 9.

[34] Hugh White was the principal author of the 2000 Defence White Paper. He is currently the director of the Australian Strategic Policy Institute.

[35] Hugh White, "Bigger not always better in Defence" Sydney Morning Herald [On-Line] http://www.smh.com.au/. Accessed 7 Jan 04.

[36] "Australia unveils 10-year plan to upgrade defence fleet" *Asia Pacific News*, 07 November 2003, [On-line]; available from: http://asia.news.yahoo.com/031107/afp/031107080920asiapacificnews html

The latest strategic guidance by Government is the approved Defence Capability Review 2003.[37] As highlighted by the Minister, this review details a number of capability changes aligned with Defence Update 2003. In relation to force structure, the review identifies an increased requirement to strengthen the effectiveness and sustainability of the Army, to provide air defense protection to deploying forces, to enhance the lift requirement for deployments, and position forces to exploit emerging Network Centric Warfare advantages.[38]

The review states that Army must become more sustainable and lethal in close combat. In order to provide Army with the combat weight required to be more sustainable, means the replacement of Australia's ageing Leopard tanks.[39] While the review recognizes the added complexity of unconventional threats,[40] one belief is that Army will transform into a mobile, flexible force to fight alongside the United States in conflicts across the globe.[41] While the review stipulates capability investment, a recurring theme in Australian defense policy is prevalent: the need for flexibility and adaptability increases as certainty and predictability decrease.[42] This suggests that flexibility and adaptability are key facets for any force structure initiative and the ability for the Australian Army to best serve the nation.

The Debate on Force Structure

Despite Government efforts to articulate strategic direction for the ADF, contrasting perspectives exist throughout Defence circles. This spirited debate exists due to contrasting

---

[37] The Defence Capability Review Statement 2003 is not a published document. It was released by the Australian government 07 Nov 03, [On-line] ; available from Mediacentre@defence.gov.au

[38] ibid: no page no.

[39] ibid: no page no.

[40] Aldo Borgu, The Defence Capability Review 2003: A Modest and Incomplete Review. Australian Strategic Policy Institute, Canberra, 2003, 3.

[41] Mark Forbes, "Australia – US Defence Ties Set to Widen," *The Melbourne Age,* 27 February 2003. [On-line]: http://www.theage.com.au/articles/2003/02/26/1046064105879 html Accessed:[07 November 2003]. For comments rebutting this perception See: Chief of the Australian Army, LTG Peter Leahy. "A Land Force for the Future: The Australian Army in the Early 21ˢᵗ Century." *Australian Army Journal,* vol. 1. (June 2003): 19-28.

[42] Forbes, "Australia – US Defence Ties Set to Widen," 2003.

beliefs that govern force structure and how this should best serve the nation. Debate exists

between whether defending interests that may be global should drive force structure of Army, or

should it remain structured for DOA? The CA states that there cannot be an 'either / or' choice.

Australia must embrace the combined yes response to the dialectic that exists between Australia's

interests and Australia's geography.[43]

Former Australian Defence Minister, Peter Reith argues that after 100 years, it is time

Australia grew out of the 'intellectual straitjacket'. Australia should move away from having to

choose between DOA and active engagement in regional strategic affairs towards embracing both

options.[44] The current Defence Minister who states "It probably never made sense to

conceptualize our security interests as a series of diminishing concentric circles around our

coastline, but it certainly does not do so now" supports this view.[45]

While there may be some merit in the view of defense experts who remain fixated that

the ADF should be structured for DOA because all other calls for the ADF can be adopted from

this force structure, this historical factor should not dominate opinion.[46] A more current,

prescriptive and holistic view is that Australia's limited resources and the extent of its geography

and regional interests mean that Australia's armed forces must be balanced, flexible, multi-

purpose and sustainable.[47] Force structure planning should therefore be based on similar

principles.[48]

---

[43] Leahy "A Land Force for the Future: The Australian Army in the Early 21st Century." 19-20.

[44] Peter Reith "The Blamey Oration." *Australian Defence Force Journal,* vol 149 (Jul/Aug 2001)

[45] Senator Robert Hill, Minister for Defence, 'Beyond the White Paper: Strategic Directions for Defence', Address to the Australian Defence College, Canberra, 18 June 2002. Hill's remark was a transparent allusion to the map featured in the 1987 Dibb Report, depicting a series of concentric circles radiating outwards from Australia, indicating the radii of potential threats to the continental heartland.

[46] S.D. Evans, "The Defence of Australia and its' Interests." *Australian Defence Force Journal,* vol. 143 (Jul/Aug 2000): 31

[47] Michael Wyndham Hudson. "Australian Government's Major Responsibilities and the Principles Underlying Defence Force Development." *Australian Defence Force Journal,* vol. 143 (Jul/Aug 2000): 40.

[48] Michael O'Connor. "Crafting a National Defence Policy." *Australian Defence Force Journal,* vol. 143 (Jul/Aug 2000): 45.

In a recent speech, the CA stated that the Government regards the likelihood of a direct, conventional, military attack on the Australian mainland by a hostile nation as extremely low. DOA is no longer going to be the influential determinant of our force structure.[49] In the future, advanced armies are likely to field modular, task force oriented formations with smaller, high-tempo, lethal, and agile units able to attack from many directions. Under modular organization, formations may become more self-contained with a "golf bag of capabilities" to draw upon.[50]

National Interests

The Army must be a highly flexible organization if it is to serve the broad and dynamic demands of national interests.[51] The Australian Government employs the Army on missions where a land warfighting capability is necessary to achieve a desired national objective. The broad range of possible scenarios which land warfighting capacity is likely to be required is expressed as a Spectrum of Conflict in Figure 1.[52]

---

[49] Lieutenant General Peter Leahy, AO, Address to the Australian Command and General Staff College, Canberra, 25 March 2003, [On-line] ; available from www.defence.gov.au/army

[50] Michael Evans. "Fabrizio's Choice: Organisational Change and the Revolution in Military Affairs Debate." *Australian Defence Force Journal*, vol. 44 (Sep/Oct 2000): 86.

[51] Australian Department of Defence *Future Warfighting Concept,* 5.

[52] See: The Spectrum of Operations. Australian Department of Defence. *Force 2020.* Canberra, Australia: National Capital printing, 2002 for further details. *FORCE 2020* recognizes that Australia will increasingly be involved across the full spectrum of operations, with the defense of Australian National interests as the Army's core business. *FORCE 2020* defines the 'spectrum of operations' as extending from assisting with emergency relief to matters of national survival. The approach is underpinned by the concept of 'likelihood versus consequence' where operations to the left of the spectrum are more likely, but their consequences are relatively limited. The reverse is true for those operations to the right of the spectrum, where although they might be relatively unlikely, the consequences may be catastrophic for Australia.

Figure 1. The Spectrum of Operations. Australian Department of Defence. Force 2020. Canberra, Australia: National Capital printing, 2002: 9.

For Army to best serve Australian national interests its force structure should be balanced, flexible and adaptive. Balance is the essential factor for any transformed Army force and was the basis for the decision to upgrade the Army's tank capability. As highlighted by Senator Hill, the key to the tank argument is the desire to achieve a balanced force that is able to deal with unconventional threats like terrorism, and enhance Australia's ability in an uncertain and complex environment.[53] The recent success of the US Abrams tanks during OIF has also influenced the Australian Government.[54] The Australian strategic relationship with the US is a critical element of Australian strategic policy and national interests.[55]

---

[53] Max Blenkin "Tanks for the effort: Senator" *Daily Telegraph*, November 8, 2003, [On-line] ; available from http://dailytelegraph.news.com.au/printerfriendly.jsp?sectionid=1260&storyid=456239

[54] Tom Allard, "Military will get the Might for Large Operations Abroad" *Sydney Morning Herald* (Sydney) 8 November 2003, [Online] ; available from http://www.smh.com.au/

[55] Statements and actions by the government over the past 18 months indicate that the US influence for Australian Defense is vital. Senator Hill stated in a speech " Australia's alliance with the United States is a major strategic asset. It contributes directly to our own security. It adds to our strategic weight and capability edge in the region, and our ability to protect our interests. And it gives us access and influence in Washington out of all proportion to our size. This enhances our ability to pursue our international political, security and economic interests more broadly." For further details See: Senator Robert Hill, Minister for Defence, "US Grand Strategy: Implications for Alliance partners" Speech to the Defence and Strategic Studies Centre, Hyatt Hotel, Canberra Friday, 1 August 2003, [On-line] ; available from http://www.defence.gov.au/adc/conference_papers/minister%20robert%20hill.doc

Alliances

"Australia's longstanding partnership with the United States is of fundamental importance. The depth of security, economic and political ties that we have with the United States makes this a vital relationship. No other country can match the United States' global reach in international affairs. Further strengthening Australia's ability to influence and work with the United States is essential for advancing our national interests. Australia and the United States share values and ideals that underpin our strong relationship. We both have deep democratic traditions and aspirations, elements of a common heritage and a lasting record of cooperation and shared sacrifice. Our security alliance is a practical manifestation of these shared values. It is the centerpiece of a much broader relationship in which the United States is our largest foreign investor and largest single trading partner. The extent of shared interests gives us considerable scope to cooperate bilaterally and internationally to achieve better outcomes for us both."[56]

Strategic alliances, especially with the US, play an important role in Australian defense policy and associated force structure initiatives. The ANZUS alliance has proven its continuing relevance to shared security interests. For example the US provided valuable logistics and personnel support to the Australian-led multinational force in East Timor. Similarly invoking the ANZUS treaty (first time), and the deployment of Australian forces to OIF and OEF reflect how important the Australian –US alliance is to Australia. [57]

The global-ambiguous threat based environment will continue to place an emphasis on security relationships such as that with the US. This does not imply a total dominance by the US or that Australian interests are purely driven by the US. [58] Belief in such a statement is wrong.

---

[56] Australian Department of Foreign Affairs and Trade. *Australian Foreign and Trade Policy White Paper: Advancing the National Interests*, Canberra, Australia: National Capital Printing 2003:86.

[57] Ibid., 89.

[58] A common theme expressed in media print over the past 2 months is that Force structure initiates within Australia will be dominated by the US. The likely purchase of the replacement US Abrams Tanks is one example where critics see an over dominance by US relations. Critics of the tank proposal include the head of the Australian Strategic Policy Institute, Hugh White, who believes the Defence money would be better spent elsewhere including on more troops. Other comments reflect that a purchase of a new tank is yet again another blind message to support an Australian-US blind alliance that does not reflect true national interests. Current Strategic policy *Defence Update 2003* directs otherwise, as Australian Force structure initiatives will be continually influenced by the relationship with the US and standardization programs such as the ABCA (America Britain, Canada, Australia and New Zealand). For contrasting perspectives on new tanks or reliance on the US see Hugh White "Bigger not always better in Defence." *Herald Sun*, 24 November 2003 [On-line]; available from http://www.smh.com.au/articles/2003/11/23/1069522471202.html?from=storyrhs

The Australian Government will continue to pursue interests even if views differ from the US. "In this regard, the very close bilateral relationship is an important asset in the Government's advocacy of Australian interests."[59]

Coalition interoperability will continue as an important design factor for the Australian Army, particularly with the US. This facet should not cloud priorities or bias understandings.[60] Aspects from US transformation can however provide valuable insights for Australian Army force designers.[61] Further discussion on the US alliance and US approach to warfare is in Chapter 3.

Other important alliances range from Australia's historical relationship with New Zealand through to regional and technological interests with France. New Zealand is Australia's most important ally in the South Pacific region. Australia's military history, heritage and traditions with New Zealand are rich. Both countries share the ANZAC traditions, from the beaches of Gallipoli (WWI), the jungles of Vietnam (Battle of Long Tan in Vietnam); through to the recent valuable contributions made by New Zealand in East Timor, Bougainville and the Solomon Islands.[62] This strong relationship will continue.

Important alliances with many European countries also influence Australian policy. The UK, Denmark, France, Germany, Ireland, Italy, Norway and Portugal all provided significant personnel, military hardware and financial contributions to the Australian-led INTERFET

---

[59] Australian Department of Foreign Affairs and Trade. *Australian Foreign and Trade Policy White Paper: Advancing the National Interests*, 2003:86.

[60] A recent article stated: "Senator Hill has emphasized the need for interoperability with the US, and an Australian fleet of Abrams would facilitate easy training interchange between the two forces and access to ongoing development. It could also allow Australian crews to fight in pre-positioned US tanks." Mark Forbes, "Australia – Australia Leaning to $600 Million US Muscle Tanks" *The Melbourne Age,* 20 November 2003 [On-line]; available from www.theage.com.au/articles/2003/11/19/1069027187696 html

[61] Us Guidance states that "a key aspect of operating force transformation is to achieve significantly improved joint and coalition force integration and interoperability." Establish Mil-to-Mil engagements through programs such as ABCA allow both Armies the ability to standardize developments and develop working systems to base future coalition alignments. United States Joint Forces Command, *Joint Transformation Roadmap, 03 November 2003,* (Washington D.C: Government Printing Office, 2003), 17.

operation in East Timor. In addition, the UK, France and Germany are important sources of Defence technology, such as the Hawk Trainer Aircraft and the Franco-German Tiger armed reconnaissance helicopter recently purchased by Australia. Regionally, a trilateral agreement exists with France (and New Zealand) to cooperate on disaster relief operations in the South Pacific.[63] The complex global environment creates connectivity between a multitude of regional and global alliances that will continue to play an important role in Australian strategic policy. Force structure initiatives must cater for such diversity in order to serve Australian interests.

---

[62] Australian Department of Foreign Affairs and Trade. *Australian Foreign and Trade Policy White Paper: Advancing the National Interests*, 2003:91.
    [63] Ibid., 99.

CHAPTER THREE

THE CURRENT AUSTRALIAN ARMY FORCE STRUCTURE AND REASON FOR CHANGE

"Australia's interests are global in scope and not solely defined by geography" Australian Department of Foreign Affairs and Trade (DFAT), *Advancing the National Interest*, 2003.

"The new strategic environment requires a more flexible and mobile force, with sufficient levels of readiness and sustainability to meet the challenges of these uncertain times". Department of Defence, Defence *Update*, 2003.

"In near term there is less likely to be a need for ADF operations in defence of Australia". Speech by the Minister for Defence, Senator Hill, 26 February 2003.

"The new strategic environment requires a more flexible and mobile force, with sufficient levels of readiness and sustainability to meet the challenges of these uncertain times". Defence Update 2003.

Current Australian Army Force Structure

The current Australian Army force structure is available from the Australian Army public

website.[64] From a ground maneuver perspective, the conventional structure includes: two regular

brigade headquarters (one mechanized and one light), a tank regiment (Leopard I),

reconnaissance regiment (LAV), one mechanized battalion (M113A1), two APC Squadrons

(M113A1)[65], three light infantry battalions, and one parachute battalion.[66] A simplified

breakdown of Australian regular forces is at Appendix B. For the purpose of this paper, emphasis

will focus on the highlighted conventional ground maneuver assets indicated in this appendix.

---

[64] Chart available [On-line] from Australian Army Public Website; http://www.defence.gov.au/army/organisation/05052003ArmyOrgChartInternet.pdf. This chart includes the Army HQ, Land Command Forces, and Training Command Forces that are both Regular and Army Reserve. For further details regarding the Australian Army force structure see the Defence Capability fact book at http://www.defence.gov.au/publications/cfb.pdf

[65] Each APC squadron is capable of lifting a total of 2 infantry companies, one specialist platoon and an infantry battalion tactical headquarters.

[66] Ground force also includes the Special Forces group that will not be addressed in this monograph. This group includes: the Special Air Service regiment (SAS), a commando battalion and an incident response regiment (High Risk Engineer Search, NBC and explosive ordinance disposal unit).

A simplified version of these ground maneuver assets is represented in Figure 2.

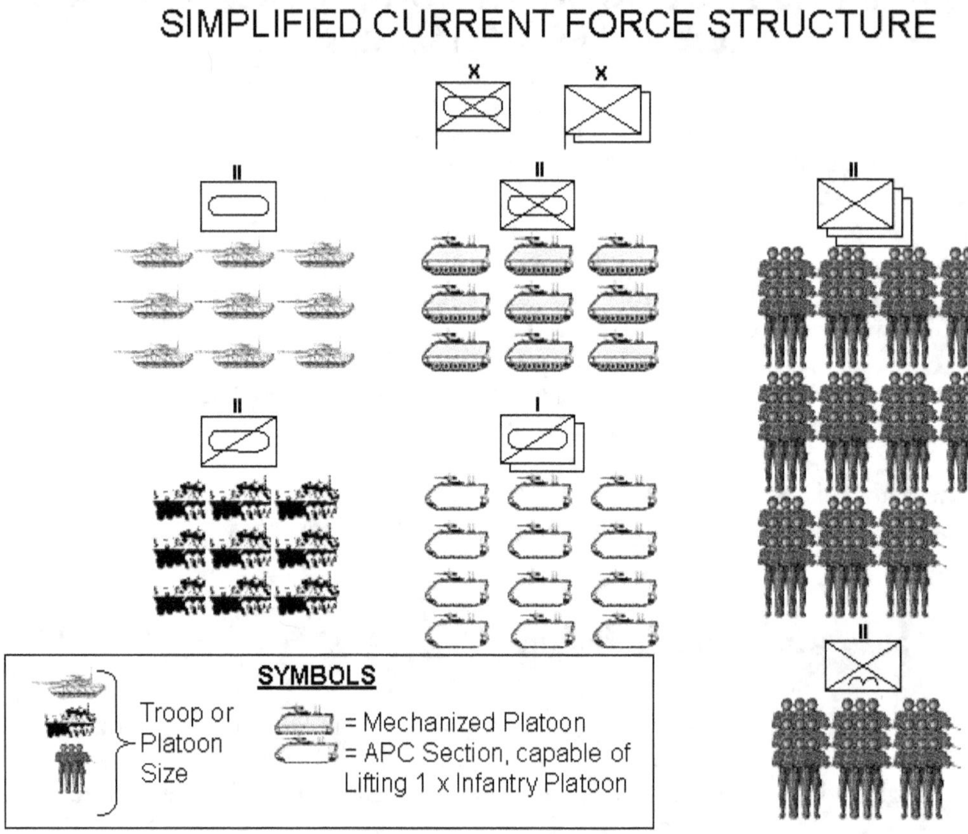

SIMPLIFIED CURRENT FORCE STRUCTURE

Figure 2 - Simplified Current Force Structure

Analysis of any Army's force structure demands an examination of the nature of war. History has proved that a nation's approach to future warfare significantly influences its ability to effect change. The Germans reaction to their defeat in WW I resulted in a revolutionary approach to war that emphasized maneuver and armored warfare. From a holistic perspective, France and England failed to learn these lessons and misunderstood the nature of future warfare resulting in inadequate preparation for the opening battles of WWII.[67] Using history as a guide, arguably, the

---

[67] Williamson Murray and Allan R. Millet ed., *Military Innovation in the Interwar Period* (Cambridge UK. Cambridge University Press 1996), 7.

combatant who understands the nature of war, has the capability to cope with the complexities of conflict and exploit it, will have a decided advantage.[68]

Future Warfighting Concepts

"It would be a mistake to underrate our enemies because they do not possess all of our technology or share our belief system. The events of 11 September 2001 and the Bali bombing of 12 October 2002 demonstrated that it is possible for those enemies to do us great harm armed only with box-cutters or bombs made with garden fertilizer".[69]

"While terrorists and criminals have demonstrated an impressive and sometimes lethal capacity to perpetrate violence they seldom do so in conventional ways. They have no armored divisions, aircraft carriers or squadrons of advanced fighter aircraft at their disposal. But they fight asymmetrically, using surprise, deception, detailed planning, networking and the selected use of advanced technology as well as cruder instruments of violence to combat the generally superior firepower at the disposal of the states they seek to undermine." [70]

The environment in which the Australian Army will be required to fight is increasingly complex and demanding. The complexity of this environment includes: physical, cultural, civil, technological, political, moral, ethical and legal challenges. Added to the complexities already listed are the issues of limited personnel, financial and equipment resources, and Australia's desire to be a global citizen not just a regional player. The understanding and identification of this complex environment is reflected in two key Australian publications: *Future Warfighting Concept* 2003; and *Complex Warfighting* (Draft version 3.2) Oct 2003.

The Future Land Warfare (FLW) paper, *Complex Warfighting,* specifies that globalization is the key driver of the non-linear and non-contiguous complex environment.[71] As a

---

[68] Christopher D. Kolenda. "Transforming How We Fight." *Naval War College Review*, Vol LVI, No. 2. (Spring 2003), 108.
[69] Alan Ryan *Putting Your Young Men in the Mud.* Study Paper no. 124, Land Warfare Studies Centre, Duntroon, Canberra, Australia, November 2003:8
[70] Alan Dupont. "Transformation or Stagnation? Rethinking Australia's Defence." *Australian Journal of International Affairs.* Vol. 57 (April 2003): 64.
[71] Future Warfighting Concept describes the battle space as a linear concept of 'battlefield' which is changing to encompass a broader range of environments, which include maritime, aerospace, land, electromagnetic, information, temporal, social and political dimensions where conflict is fought. The non-linear nature of the battle space is seen in the way that seemingly small changes can have a huge influence

result, Australia can no longer classify national interests from a perspective coterminous with territory. Creative approaches to protect these interests must be examined.

Success in this environment will depend on the application of flexible and discriminating forces, whose structure may be small, semi-autonomous, modular or even from morphing organizations. Organizations will need to be developed on Australia's continued interest in an effects-based-approach, where a whole of government effort, will influence populations and perceptions.[72]

Complex Warfighting also states: "that while there are some new elements in the external conflict environment, there are enduring continuities between previous forms of warfare and the types of conflict now appearing. These continuities represent enduring trends that have been characteristic of warfare for millennia – complexity, diversity, diffusion and lethality."[73] Fog and friction will continue to complicate the environment and adversaries will be formed from contrasting backgrounds and interests.[74] Future adversaries will less likely be state based and more likely to include: insurgents, guerrillas, partisans or ex-members of a defeated regular force, terrorists or even organized criminals.[75]

Complexity will also be enhanced by the very nature of the battle space. The enduring character of warfare will continue to shape and reshape adding further complexity to the non-linear battle space to the point where the 'conventional' and 'unconventional' aspects of conflict

---

on events and vice versa. It also reflects the different and unconventional means that adversaries will pursue and adopt to achieve their aims. The non-linear battle space is also non-contiguous, where interrelated operations could occur in any part of the world simultaneously or with a significant time lag between such operations.

[72] Australia Department of Defence. *Complex Warfighting* (Draft version 3.2). Canberra, Australia: Future Land Warfare Branch, Oct 2003:12-15.

[73] Ibid., 4.

[74] Operation Iraqi Freedom demonstrated the enduring uncertainty of war and thoroughly discredited portions of the US Service and US Joint Visions based on the assumption of near-certainty. It was clear before the war began that RMA technology had neither lifted the fog of war nor provided the capability to achieve quick, cheap and decisive victory in Iraq. The key to victory in Iraqi Freedom was the joint capability that the coalition employed to impose its will on the enemy. See: H.R. McMaster, Crack in the Foundation: Defense Transformation and the Underlying Assumption of Dominant Knowledge in Future War, Center for Strategic Leadership, Us Army War College, Carlisle PA. November 2003: 84-86.

will be difficult to separate. These factors will influence the tactics, and possibly the strategy of the Australian Army and at the same time influence the behavior of potential adversaries.[76]

Australia's approach to warfighting will continue to be shaped by globalization of the international system, the strategic pre-eminence of the US, the increasing role of non-state actors, and the enduring factors of both chaos and uncertainty.[77] The objective nature of war, regardless of where or when, will always include the elements of violence, friction, chance and uncertainty.[78] Force constructs or theories must be cognizant of such factors and structure accordingly.

US Approach to future Warfare

The pre-eminence of the United States, will shape the future battle space and continue to play a key role in Australian defense strategies and national interests. US transformation, technological developments, facets of interoperability will continue to influence actions and policy of the Australian Government. Access to US information and technology play a significant role in enhancing Australia's defense capability, making the relationship with the United States a national asset.[79]

As reflected by Defence Minister Hill, with a decreased risk of conventional military attack, Australia needs a reshaped force to join US-led coalitions against terrorism.[80] Australia's commitment of military forces to operations in Afghanistan and Iraq highlight Australia's

---

[75] Australia Department of Defence. *Complex Warfighting* (Draft version 3.2) 2003:5.

[76] Australian Department of Defence. *Future Warfighting Concept.* Canberra, Australia: National Capital printing, 2003: 8.

[77] Ibid., 6.

[78] Antulio J. Echevarria II, *Globalization and the Nature of War.* Strategic Studies Institute, U.S. War College, Carlisle Barracks PA. 2003: 7.

[79] *Australia's National Security: A Defence Update 2003,* 9.

[80] Mark Forbes, "Australia – US Defence Ties Set to Widen," *The Melbourne Age,* 27 February 2003, [On-line]; available from: www.theage.com.au/articles/2003/02/26/1046064105879.html

commitment to such actions.[81] They also expose shortfalls within the military, as evidenced by the limited acceptable options Army could provide the Australian Government. As highlighted in the US National Security Strategy, the US military must transform in order to provide the President with a wider range of military options to discourage aggression and any form of coercion against the United States. [82]

Similar initiatives are required within Australia. Not just to provide Government with options, but to also spread the operational weight across a broader portion of the force and not just niche capabilities like SF. It is therefore prudent for the Australian Army to keep abreast of any initiatives or change adopted by either the US Army or US Marine Corps.

US military analysts are concerned with a perceived over-dependency that the US transformation concept invests in technology. They see the danger of a continued focus almost exclusively on technology is that US armed forces risk developing strategies, force structures and war fighting concepts that are at odds with the nature of war. [83] US Army Chief of Staff, General Schoomaker believes that the US Army lost its way on the path to relevance and readiness after the Cold War. He has initiated sixteen focus areas to get the Army back on track, his top four being: taking care of the soldier; develop a joint and expeditionary mindset, restructuring the force to attain relevant balance; and develop modularity (smaller, agile building block units).[84]

The USMC emphasize the "timeless realities of human conflict" over any technological factors. While technology will influence the future battlefield, it will not dominate. History

---

[81] The Australian Government deployed a 1000 man contingent (based on a SAS squadron) to Operation Enduring Freedom OEF and a 2000 man composite task force (also based on a SAS squadron) to Operation Iraqi Freedom (OIF).

[82] U.S. Department of Defense, *Military Transformation: A Strategic Approach.* [On-line]; available from http://www.oft.osd.mil/library/library_files/document_297_MT_StrategyDoc1.pdf.

[83] Kolenda. "Transforming How We Fight." 2003, 102.

[84] One example of General Schoomaker's approach to a "modular force" is the direction he gave to 101ˢᵗ Airbourne Division to create five brigade structures form the current three infantry brigades, the artillery brigade and the engineer brigade. Notes from 34th Annual IFPA / Fletcher School Conference: Security Planning & Military Transformation After Iraqi Freedom, 2-3 DEC 03 at US Chamber of Commerce Building, Washington, DC. Conference Notes emailed by LTCOL Richard Dixon, G3 CAC HQ Fort Leavenworth (Richard.Dixon@us.army.mil) 4 Jan 2004.

teaches us that major transformations in warfare are rare, and are triggered by more than one major technological breakthrough.[85] Using Clausewitz, the USMC define the nature of war as: "a violent struggle between hostile, independent, irreconcilable wills characterized by chaos, friction, and uncertainty". Such factors will remain unchanged as they transcend advancements in technology.[86]

The USMC Marine Corps doctrine has also introduced the widely accepted theory of the 'three-block war'. This theory states that:

> "Humanitarian assistance operations, peace operations, and full-scale, high-intensity combat may occur simultaneously in different neighborhoods. Integrating and coordinating these various evolutions, each of which has its own peculiarities, will challenge Marines to use their skill and determination in innovative and imaginative ways."[87]

This notion of simultaneous intensities presents further complexity to the force designer. In many ways, force composition for what is perceived to be a benign environment must be capable of intense close combat.

Australian philosophy is similar to current US Army and Marine perspectives. Regardless of technological or strategic conditions, some aspects of the battle space will endure. War will remain chaotic. This chaos, which is produced by the complex way that friction and the fog of war interact, can only be managed by the determined application of human will and intellect. People will therefore remain the most important element of ADF capability.[88]

Australia's participation in US led coalitions in Afghanistan and Iraq has had significant impacts on its outlook. Australian observations of US actions are important because:

---

[85] Huba Wass de Czege *"New Paradigm" Tactics: A Primer on the Transformation of Land Power* Emailed by LTC Richard Dixon [richard.dixon@us.army.mil], G3 CAC HQ, US Army Fort Leavenworth, 24 Oct 2003, 8.

[86] H.R. McMaster, Crack in the Foundation: Defence Transformation and the Underlying Assumption of Dominant Knowledge in Future War, Center for Strategic Leadership, Us Army War College, Carlisle PA. November 2003.

[87] United States Marine Corps, *Warfighting Concepts for the 21st Century*, Marine Corps Combat Development Command, Quantico, VA, 1996, p. VII-5.

[88] Australian Department of Defence. *Future Warfighting Concept.* 2003: 9.

> "What died on the battlefields of Iraq was the vision held by many of a homogenized army—one in which units would largely resemble one another. Instead, the army of the future will require a large kit bag of capabilities that it can deploy and fit together, sometimes in the middle of battle, to meet the many exigencies of this new era in warfare. For example, in the open battlefield, lighter forces equipped with new information systems proved highly effective at engaging and destroying the Iraqis. But speed and information superiority became less decisive when combat occurred at closer range, as in the complex urban terrain of Basra and Baghdad. There, older weapons systems such as the Abrams and Bradley, with their advantages in protection, mass, and explosive power, proved to be of considerable utility. This traditional machine-age equipment is likely to remain a part of ground forces in the future."[89]

Comparisons between Australia and the US tend to reflect the perception that there are many facets of military change only possible in the US, due to its military's mass, scale, and size. This is not true because Australian thinking, while more conservative, seeks the same transformation advantages.[90]

Opinion and Perspectives within the Defence Community

> "Our current strategy has four major deficiencies. It is based on a misplaced geographical determinism that ignores the diverse and globalised nature of modern conflict; it has shaped the ADF for the wrong wars; it gives insufficient weight to the transnational threats which confront us; and it fails to recognize that modern defense forces must win the peace as well as the war."[91]

While there are contrasting opinions within Defence circles regarding future warfare and force structure requirements of the military, one common thread exists; the Army must change to meet new demands.[92] Looking at the recent experiences of Iraq, popular belief amongst Defence circles is: Canberra wanted to make a far more significant contribution to Iraq (OIF) than it did in Afghanistan (OEF), however no credible and acceptable military option existed for

---

[89] Robert H Scales MG (Ret) *Statement to the House Armed Services Committee, US House of Representatives*, 21 October 2003, Washington DC: [On-line] available from http://www.iwar.org.uk/news-archive/iraq/lessons-learned/03-10-21-scales html.

[90] Christopher Flaherty "The relevance of the US Transformation Paradigm for the Australian Defence Force." *Defence and Security Analysis.* Vol 19 No 3 (September 2003): 240.

[91] Alan Dupont. "Transformation or Stagnation? Rethinking Australia's Defence." *Australian Journal of International Affairs.* Vol. 57 (April 2003): 55.

[92] For additional conflicting views towards Australian Defence strategy see Monk, Paul. *Rethinking the Defence of Australia.* 2003. [Database on-line0 available from Austhink, www.austhink.org/monk/dibb htm

Government.[93] A common belief why a predominant SAS niche package was sent to Iraq is that Australia did not have a modern conventional force capable of battlefield interoperability with the US.[94] Some suggest that this situation developed because of Army's previous emphasis on a light infantry force capability against a guerrilla action in Australia's Northern Territory.[95]

Dupont argues that disparity today exists due to an incorrect investment in a maritime-based strategy at the cost of land power. "In committing so much of the defense budget to the Navy and Air Force at the expense of the Army, the 'gatekeepers of strategic doctrine' pursued a policy that severely weakened the Army's capacity for force projection in the mistaken belief that air and naval power would suffice."[96] Australia's tiny land-force contribution in Iraq exposed a longstanding and serious imbalance in Army. The Australian Army has an inability to deploy significant numbers of adequately protected troops into conflict where close combat could occur."[97]

Supporters for enhancing the Army argue that a policy for niche forces is politics on the cheap. Niche forces, such as the Australian SAS, may fit the specialized needs of a coalition force structure and reduce the risk of casualties for the Australian Government, however, what sort of political message does this send to Allies? Is Australia a staunch military ally, or possibly a political opportunist? A niche force may satisfy the political demands of showing the Australian flag internationally, at the lowest possible cost to gain the maximum strategic and political kudos,

---

[93] This opinion is a collective reflection of comments made by Alan Dupont. "Transformation or Stagnation? Rethinking Australia's Defence, John Essex-Clark, "Niche Forces: First thoughts from an Army Perspective; and various Defence articles written by Defence Journalists: Paul Vaughn, Mark Forbes, Ian McPhedran, Mark John Thompson, and Patrick Walters.

[94] John Essex-Clark, "Niche Forces: First thoughts from an Army Perspective," *Australian Army Journal.* Vol 1 (June 2003): 12.

[95] Paul Vaughn, "Australia Warms Towards Bargain Leopard 2A4 MBTs" *Asia-pacific Defence Reporter,* (July/August 2003): 6.

[96] Alan Dupont. "Transformation or Stagnation? Rethinking Australia's Defence." 2003: 58-59. Dupont also argues that that the conceptual weakness of the Defence of Australia (DOA) doctrine is that it is based on a notion of threat that takes little account of the declining strategic relevance of geography and the proliferation of non-military, non-state challenges to security.

[97] Patrick Walters "Australia's Army has been degraded by successive Governments..." *The Weekend Australian,* 4-5 October 2003, p23.

however what effect does this have on real war-fighting capability. The Australian Army will be unable to operate across the full spectrum of potential operations if it adopts a niche force approach to future warfighting.[98] While niche forces offer advantages, Government needs broader options.

A balanced, self-reliant, and ready ADF able to complete a wide range of capabilities in tomorrow's complex warfare environment is not possible under the current structure.[99] "The Australian Army may be seen as high quality, however it is very small and ill equipped for substantial land force operations against capable adversaries."[100] While niche forces offer advantages, the Australian Government must have options.[101] If the need exists for a flexible, versatile, modular, and more agile force to serve a whole-of-government approach to Australian national interests, and deal with a broad range of non-traditional threats, then force structure changes must occur to reflect this.[102]

---

[98] John Essex-Clark, "Niche Forces: First thoughts from an Army Perspective," *Australian Army Journal.* Vol 1 (June 2003): 15.

[99] Richard G. Wilson *Australia's Defence Review 2000: A step in the Right Direction.* U.S. Army War College Strategy Research Project, U.S. War College, Carlisle Barracks PA. 2001: 2.

[100] Mark John Thompson, *Pay your Money and Take your Pick: Defence Spending Choices for Australia.* December 2003. The Australian Strategic Policy Institute [Online]; available from http://www.aspi.org.au/paymoney/index html

[101] John Essex-Clark, "Niche Forces: First thoughts from an Army Perspective," 2003: 14.

[102] Greg de Somer, The Implications of the United States Army's Army-After-Next: Concepts for the Australian Army. (Duntroon, Canberra, Australia: Land Warfare Studies Centre 1999), 15.

CHAPTER FOUR

THE 'HARDENING' CONCEPT

"Given changes in technology, capabilities, Australia's geo-political situation and guidance from the Australia Government, the Army of today is not the Army we require tomorrow. We need to consider hardening and networking the Army, seeking to improve our protection, mobility and firepower and our ability to work in a joint and combined environment."[103]

The Chief of the Australian Army (CA), Lieutenant General Peter Leahy's answer to the challenges of globalization and complex warfare is a 'hardened Army'.[104] In order to become 'harder,' the Army must be better protected, able to hit harder, more agile and more closely integrated into Joint and Coalition frameworks. Using observations from operations in Afghanistan, Iraq, and East Timor, the CA stated that: "Army must move from a light infantry force to a light armored force with increased protection, firepower and mobility. The alternative is for us to steadily lose capability over time as existing systems age and are overwhelmed by the emerging threat environment."[105]

The CA describes the hardened force as being mobile, agile, flexible and versatile.[106] Army force structure will need to embrace the characteristics of rapid deployment, adaptability and flexibility, otherwise it will be incapable of serving the nations vital interests.[107] In the past five years, the expansion of the Army's role beyond the traditional DOA has been Army's greatest challenge.[108] The environment has changed, and now so must Army.

---

[103] Lieutenant General Peter Leahy, AO, Address to the United Service Institution of the Australian Capital Territory, Australia , 11 June 2003, [On-line] ; available from www.defence.gov.au/

[104] Lieutenant General Peter Leahy, AO, Address to the Land Warfare Conference, 28 October 2003, [On-line] ; available from www.defence.gov.au/army. In his speech Lieutenant General Leahy, states that the Army's response to the challenges posed by Complex War Fighting and Government guidance, must be met by a 'harder Army'. As such, he has directed within Army a process called 'hardening'. He sees this process as being critical for future Army success on the future battlefield.

[105] Lieutenant General Peter Leahy, AO, Address to the United Service Institution of the Australian Capital Territory, Australia , 11 June 2003, [On-line]; available from www.defence.gov.au/army

[106] John Kerin "$25 Bn defence Review: A fit out for US service" *The Weekend Australian,* 4-5 October 2003, p2.

[107] Peter Leahy "A Land Force for the Future: The Australian Army in the Early 21st Century." *Australian Army Journal.* Vol 1. (June 2003): 27.

[108] Ibid., 19.

Using Army concepts of warfare,[109] the key to Army's credibility and effectiveness will be its ability for complex warfighting and close combat.[110] Warfare has moved beyond the concept of the 'three block war'[111] to what is termed 'Complex War Fighting'. Force design planners must embrace this critical design factor. "The diffusion of lethality, especially to non state entities, means that apparently benign missions can rapidly escalate into intense combat."[112] The extreme complexity created by the confluence of unpredictability, lethality, diffusion, rapid transitions and diversity will dominate the future cluttered volatile and fluid battle space. The response must be a hardened Army with increased firepower linked to greater situational awareness.[113]

The combined arms team serves as the fundamental building block for the 'hardened Army'.[114] The CA also states: "a direct fire protected mobility platform (the tank) represents an important building block of both the combined arms team and a hardened networked Army. It can provide more options in terms of communications and sensors than any existing system."[115] The traditional understanding of combined elements teams has changed.

Combined arms teams must be smaller and more responsive than the company group or tank squadron traditionally regarded as the smallest building block of the combined arms

---

[109] Australia Department of Defence. *Complex Warfighting* 2003.

[110] Patrick Walters "Australia's Army has been degraded by successive Governments..." *The Weekend Australian,* 4-5 October 2003, p23.

[111] United States Marine Corps, *Warfighting Concepts for the 21st Century*, Marine Corps Combat Development Command, Quantico, VA, 1996, p. VII-5.

[112] LTG Peter Leahy, Chief of the Australian Army, Minute OCA/OUT/2003/1457, *Hardening the Army*, dated 29 August 2003, 1.

[113] LTGEN Leahy states that Complex warfighting is more intense, more diverse and more compressed spatially and temporally, and requiring quite different responses. Julian Kerr, "Army Focus on Close Combat and Hardening" A*sia-Pacific Defence Reporter*, November 2003: 44-45.

[114] Leahy, Address to the United Service Institution of the Australian Capital Territory, 2003. The CA states in this speech that this combined Arms building block, includes the close collaboration of infantry, amour, artillery, engineers, and aviation supported by combat support and combat service support elements. He believes that this combined Arms structure will act as the decisive factor in winning the land battle.

[115] Ibid.,

capability.[116] "Since 1997 Army has conducted comprehensive historical, operational and experimental analysis that has identified the essential capabilities required to achieve this goal. Based on this analysis Army must fight as task forces and battle groups not brigades and battalions."[117] The recent deployment to the Solomon Islands serves as a good example of this construct.[118]

The Hardened Force Structure Proposal

The Australian Army's Future Land Warfare Directorate (FLW)[119] is responsible for developing the 'hardening concept' and force structure options for the Australian Army. FLW define the 'hardening process" as an approach to modernize the force structure of the Army to adapt to the complex nature and challenges of future warfare.[120] The proposed FLW force-structure for the "hardened concept' is currently pending Government approval. While some aspects from this concept remain classified and are unavailable for inclusion,[121] this paper is able

---

[116] Julian Kerr, "Army Focus on Close Combat and Hardening" *Asia-Pacific Defence Reporter*, (November 2003): 44-45

[117] Department of Defence- Army, Future Land Warfare Directorate, unpublished document: *Increasing Options for Government: A Harder More Capable Army.* Russell Offices, Canberra, 2003-4.

[118] The recent Australian-Led Multinational Force (Operation ANODE and HELPEM FREN) to restore order in the Solomon Islands centered on a 350-strong police element, drawn from Australia, New Zealand and the Pacific. This operation, supported by multinational forces, consisted initially of battalion group size formation and was later reduced to security element/detachment forces. See: Department of the Parliamentary Library; Research Note: *Solomon Islands,* [On-Line]; available from http://www.aph.gov.au/library/pubs/rn/2003-04/04rn04.pdf Also see http://www.defence.gov.au/opanode/ for details on Australians contributions to the Solomon Island Operations.

[119] The Army's Future Land Warfare Directorate was created in 1999 to examine future land warfare trends out to 2030. The directorate employs a 'concept-led, capability-based' philosophy to examine force initiatives best suited to the Australian Army. For more background on the Future Land Warfare Directorate and the Australian approach of a disciplined analysis of RMA concepts, see: Michael Evans. *Australia and the Revolution in Military Affairs.* Duntroon, Canberra, Australia: Land Warfare Studies Centre, Working Paper no. 115, 2001: 15-45

[120] Department of Defence- Army, Future Land Warfare Directorate, unpublished documents. *Hardening the Arm;* and *Increasing Options for Government: A Harder More Capable Army.* Russell Offices, Canberra, 2003-4.

[121] Political sensitivities prevent FLW from releasing specifics regarding the proposed hardened structure. In particular, this includes possible re-rolling of units (by name details) and the impacts from suggested change to current unit locations (by location details). This information will become publicly available once the Australian Government endorses the concept. A likely date for such endorsement is unknown.

to address the proposed structure.[122] Essentially the FLW force structure plan modernizes the Australian Army by upgrading the current in-service MBT and reorganizes the Army's M113A1 APC assets to construct a second mechanized infantry battalion[123].

The proposed hardening force structure proposal is two mechanized infantry battalions, and 3 light infantry battalions, each standardized with three rifle companies.[124] An analysis of why Army hardening upgrades the current in-service MBT and creates the second mechanized infantry battalion will now be discussed. A diagram reflecting the hardened force structure is at Figure 3.

---

[122] Director General FLW has approved the author to include the proposed force structure outline (less sensitive issues) associated with the FLW hardening proposal. Staff Officer to the Director General FLW, Major Steve Somersby informed this approval vide email [Steven.Summersby@defence.gov.au] on 15 Jan 2004.

[123] This diagram is a simplified explanation of the hardened force structure proposed by FLW. The hardened concept encompasses other aspects that enhance Army. Aspects include enhancement of amphibious capabilities to support the Army's Manoeuvre Operations in the Littoral Environment (MOLE); increased rotary wing lift capabilities, through to communications platforms to support Network-Centric-Warfare. The FLW concept supports a 2020 timeframe in support of the *Objective Force 2020* construct. The intent is to accelerate the *Objective Force* concept and achieve a hardened Army force by 2010. MOLE was developed by FLW to guide capability development of Army to be capable of operating against a variety of threats in a complex environment in Defence of Australia and the broad range of Government directed tasks either regionally or globally to support Australian Vital Interests. Department of Defence- Army, Future Land Warfare Directorate, unpublished document: *Increasing Options for Government: A Harder More Capable Army.* Russell Offices, Canberra, 2003-4.

[124] Current regular Army infantry battalions consist of either three or four riffle company structure. In addition they include a support (specialized company) and an administrative company (similar to the US Army headquarter company construct). For more details regarding the structure and history of the Australian infantry battalion see: Alan Ryan *Putting Your Young Men in the Mud.* Study Paper no. 124, Land Warfare Studies Centre, Duntroon, Canberra, Australia, November 2003.

HARDENED FORCE STRUCTURE

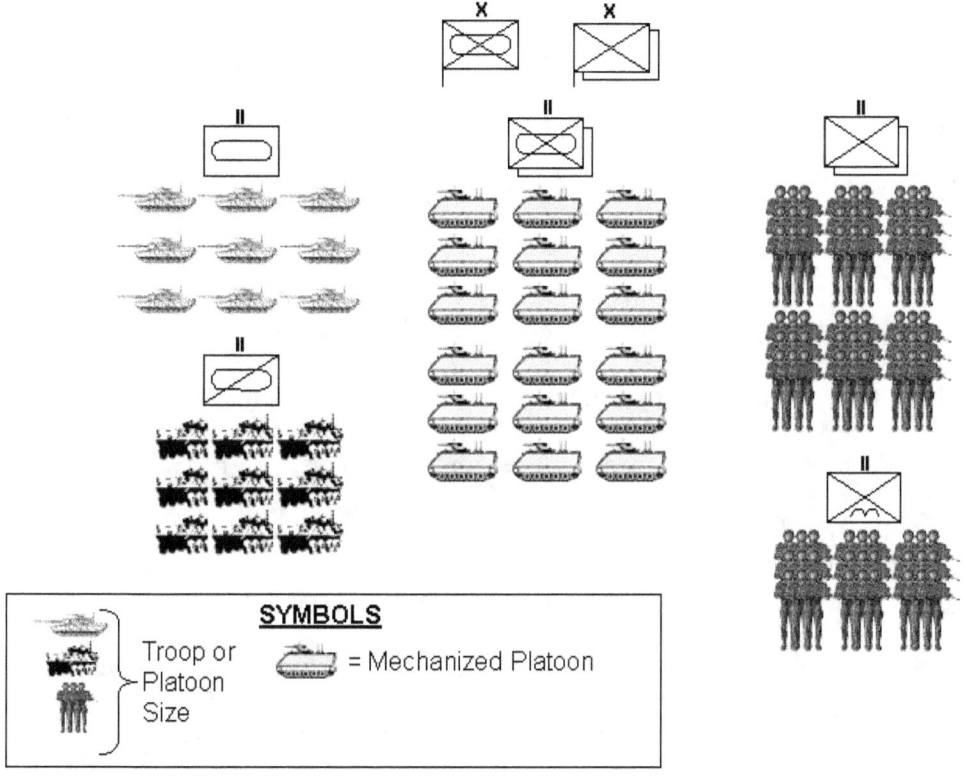

Figure 3 - Hardened Force Structure Proposal

The key to Hardening – upgrading the current in-service MBT

Research by Defence Science and Technology Organization (DSTO) concluded that the presence of tanks has the ability to significantly reduce casualties.[125]

The campaign for a replacement main battle tank (MBT) began at the Land Warfare conference in 2002. Interest then boosted following the effectiveness of heavy armor in operation in Iraq.[126] A replacement tank is key to the hardened Army concept because, from a combined arms perspective, it creates a more balanced, versatile agile and flexible force. It also presents Government with a broader range of acceptable military options. As highlighted by the CA,

---

[125] Paul Vaughn, "Australia Warms Towards Bargain Leopard 2A4 MBTs" *Asia-Pacific Defence Reporter,* (July/August 2003): 6.

[126] Julien Kerr, "Editorial Notes" *Asia-Pacific Defence Reporter,* (September 2003): 5.

British and US forces maintained momentum, and eagerly sought engagement in Iraq because they had great confidence in their armored vehicles; the Australian Army lacks such confidence.[127] The Defence Minister, Senator Hill supports this sentiment, highlighting that the Iraq war, during which Abrams tanks dominated, convinced the Australian Government of the need to buy new tanks. [128]

In complex war fighting, one cannot always expect to start from a position of advantage. An army's structure requires agile characteristics to achieve advantage. As suggested in the 'Future Warfighting Concept' the quality of agility, as a characteristic of force structure, is important because it allows a force the capability to regain the initiative.[129] A replacement tank offers this characteristic for the Australian Army.

Agility is more than regaining initiative, it also relates to adaptability and the ability to respond to changing conditions. The ability to respond requires certain mental and physical strengths. The US Army states that forces must possess the mental and physical agility to transition among the various types of operations. The tank can create such agility. Mental agility through the confidence it creates within the force and physical agility through pure physiological effects.[130]

---

[127] In a speech dated 11 Jun 03, Lieutenant General Leahy stated: the US and British forces were able to win the break-in battles in Nasiriyah and Baghdad because they could take a punch and keep hitting back- harder. Although a couple of Abrams were disabled they did not lose a single crewman to enemy anti-armored fire. Likewise, the Bradley Infantry Fighting Vehicles allowed infantry to provide vital close support in complex terrain in the classic execution of the combined arms of the close battle. Protected mobility is vital to success in the modern battle space. It is one area that the current Australian Army is deficient. Two very important lessons from Iraq support this conclusion. Lieutenant General Peter Leahy, AO, Address to the United Service Institution of the Australian Capital Territory, Australia , 11 June 2003, [On-line]; available from www.defence.gov.au/army
[128] Ian McPhedran. "50 Billion Arms Spending Spree," *The Advertiser,* 08 November 2003. [On-line]; available from http://www.theadvertiser.news.com.au/printpage/0,5942,7802420,00 html
[129] Australian Department of Defence. *Future Warfighting Concept.* 2003: 25.
[130] U.S. Department of the Army. *Objective Force,* White Paper, Government Printing Office, Washington D.C. 1999: 10.

The decision to upgrade the tank is a known policy change from the Defence 2000 White Paper.[131] Hugh White, director of the Australian Strategic Policy Institute and author of Defence 2000, believes there is no coherent strategic rationale to replace tanks unless you want to upgrade the Army's capability to take part in high-intensity OIF-style operations.[132] While it is reasonable to question the likelihood or feasibility of Australian forces operating in a high threat tank environment, the application of armor is not restricted to such contexts.[133] For the Australian Army, the upgraded tank is not about 'far flung' high intensity Iraqi style conflicts to support US coalitions; it is about capability enhancement of Australian forces that can operate in complex environments to support Australian interests across the full spectrum of operations.[134]

While the age of mass tank armies may have passed into history, the age of direct-fire armored mobility vehicles is still very much alive. For many years, infantry have been asked to assault well-defended and fortified positions in difficult terrain. If a modernized tank gives an advantage to the soldier, and protection of soldiers serves the interests of the Australian people, then arguably such capability must be reflected in the Army's force structure.[135]

The Defence Science and Technology Organization (DSTO) recently conducted research that suggests the importance of a modern tank in the complex environment. Using verifiable historical data, Robert Hall and Andrew Ross discovered that after analyzing combined arms experiences with and without tanks in Vietnam the tank significantly enhanced the agility and the

---

[131] Defence 2000 advised against the development of heavy armored forces suitable for contribution to coalition forces in high-intensity conflicts Australian Department of Defence, *Defence 2000.* Canberra, Australia: Australian Government Publishing Service, 2000: 52.

[132] Mark Forbes, Australia leaning to $600 million US Muscle Tanks, *The Age* (Melbourne) [On-Line]; available from http://www.theage.com.au

[133] Mark Forbes, "Australia – US Defence Ties Set to Widen," *The Melbourne Age,* 27 February 2003. [On-line]; available from http://www.theage.com.au/articles/2003/02/26/1046064105879 html

[134] Comments synthesized by author from Lieutenant General Peter Leahy, AO, Address to the United Service Institution of the Australian Capital Territory, Australia , 11 June 2003, [On-line]; available from www.defence.gov.au/army And Peter Leahy "A Land Force for the Future: The Australian Army in the Early 21st Century." *Australian Army Journal.* Vol 1. (June 2003): 19-20.

[135] Michael Evans and Alan Ryan ed. *From Breitenfeld to Baghdad Perspectives on Combined Arms Warfare.* Duntroon, Canberra, Australia: Land Warfare Studies Centre, Working Paper no. 122, 2003:24.

survivability of Australian soldiers. In some cases, tank support decreased the Australian casualty ratio by a factor of six. [136]

If a versatile and survivable force is critical to the Australian Government and historically of importance to the Australian people, then a replacement tank becomes a necessity not an option. In today's modern era of embedded journalists and televised warfare, force protection is essential to defend Australia's political center of gravity, its people. It is therefore impossible to overstate the importance of replacing the tank and having a capable direct fire protected mobility platform, to maintain Army's war fighting capability. [137]

> "Australian Cabinet has approved a major re-shaping of the Australian Defence Force with new army tanks and huge new amphibious ships to carry them, plus hundreds of soldiers, five or six helicopters and other equipment, across the world. "After reviewing our defence capabilities, the Government has decided to provide the ADF with new assets, equipment and capabilities that will ensure it continues to be able to defend Australian interests in an uncertain and complex environment," Senator Hill said he has structured the force for expeditionary operations in the region or around the world. [138]

The replacement tank is a direct effort to enhance the versatility, agility and flexibility of the Australian Army. Versatility across the full spectrum of operations, providing the ability to adapt quickly to unexpected operational circumstances that can occur in perceived benign environments; agility through sheer protection and physical presence; and flexibility through the multitude of capabilities the tank offers when operating in a complex environment.

Without an upgraded tank, the Australian Army may only be able to serve limited objectives associated with peacekeeping and serve limited national interests. As history has proven in operations such as Somalia, the likelihood of relatively benign environments remaining immune from the conditions of complex warfare will increasingly become questionable. The

---

[136] Ibid., 58. This study looked at post combat reports where Australian forces attacked hardened bunker style positions. Australian Forces where either dismounted, dismounted with indirect fire support or dismounted with direct fire tank support. The later case proved of considerable advantage when comparing ratios of friendly and enemy casualties.

[137] Leahy, Address to the United Service Institution of the Australian Capital Territory, Australia, 2003.

replacement tank must therefore become a standard element of Army force structure to ensure

that deployed forces are capable to react and adapt to circumstances. The Australian Government

understands such importance and, as a result, appears committed to procure a replacement tank.

Effort within Defence would best serve reinforcement of this decision by focusing effort on

which replacement tank best serves Australian needs.[139]

The Second Mechanized Infantry Battalion.

The advantages of a second mechanized battalion follow similar logic to that of a

replacement tank. The second mechanized battalion achieves greater balance and adaptability

through increased versatility, agility and orchestration[140]. Versatility is enhanced through the

ability of a communications networked and armor protected formation to rapidly adapt to changes

in operational circumstances. Agility is enhanced through an ability to rapidly transition between

tasks, smoothly and with limited guidance. Orchestration is increased through the ability to

achieve discriminating applications of force through the generation of armor protected combined

arms teams. In essence the second mechanized battalion increases the flexible muscle of Army

and adds modular flesh to the bones of the hardening concept.

To the CA the terms versatile, flexible and adaptable mean that the Australian Army must

be able to tailor mission specific groupings of infantry, amour, engineers, and aviation, with reach

---

[138] Ian McPhedran. "50 Billion Arms Spending Spree," *The Advertiser,* 08 November 2003 [On-line]; available from http://www.theadvertiser news.com.au/printpage/0,5942,7802420,00.html.
[139] The Australian government is considering two options as the replacement tank: the US Abrams M1 tank or the upgraded German built Leopard II. There are a multitude of political, capability, force transition and interoperability issues associated with such decision. Despite media comments, an agreed procurement has not been decided. Nevertheless opinions within defence and the public will become distorted with comments such as: "The Australian Defence Force is to introduce the massive American-built M1 Abrams tanks as an armored strike force to facilitate a frontline role for the army alongside the US in future international conflicts. Critics claim the 70-tonne Abrams are unsuitable for operations along crumbling Pacific roads and bridges. The tanks are too heavy to be airlifted and must be transported by sea. Hugh White, the director of the Australian Strategic Policy Institute and author of the Government's defence white paper, said he had been told that the decision to buy the Abrams "has in effect been made". The $600 million price tag was high and could be better spent on more troops for the army…" Mark Forbes, "Australia – Australia Leaning to $600 Million US Muscle Tanks" *The Melbourne Age,* 20 November 2003. [On-line]; available from www.theage.com.au/articles/2003/11/19/1069027187696 html

back to offensive support from artillery or other offensive fire support. The second mechanized battalion increases the multitude of configurations for combined arms capabilities that achieve the CA's intent. [141] For example, a second mechanized battalion provides the basis to establish a third mechanized/armor battle group within Army at high readiness. As one observation from Iraq suggests, the best means of dealing with uncertainty is the flexible employment of all-arms capabilities. [142]

The traditional mechanized structure is a robust and survivable building block for the Australian Army. Mechanized forces are agile by nature, able to execute a broad range of standard infantry-armor operations more effortless than any ad-hoc mounted force. Force organization can occur at combat team level (company/squadron), task organized to serve specific missions. Such organizations are agile enough to re-organize as the situation dictates.

In the future complex environment, Army will employ tailored combined arms teams over standard infantry style groupings. As highlighted by the CA: "the hardened Army will generate its combat power through tailored packages of combined arms teams. These will be smaller and more responsive than the combined-arms teams that we have been accustomed." [143]

Traditionally the Army has regarded the company group or squadron group as the smallest building block of combined arms capability. With the exponential improvements in lethality and connectivity that are now becoming available, that will no longer be the case." [144] Designed properly, future tactical units of employment should be re-configurable as required with

---

[140] These terms are defined in Appendix A, Method of Evaluation.

[141] Leahy, Address to the Land Warfare Conference, 28 October 2003.

[142] H.R. McMaster, Crack in the Foundation: Defense Transformation and the Underlying Assumption of Dominant Knowledge in Future War, Center for Strategic Leadership, Us Army War College, Carlisle PA. November 2003, 86.

[143] Leahy, Address to the Land Warfare Conference, 28 October 2003.

[144] Ibid.,

modular combat and combat support units, thus assuring the operational agility to conduct high-tempo operations and allowing smooth force expansion and contraction as conditions require.[145]

The mechanized structure may satisfy this design need, however there are some limitations. A mechanized battalion construct is that it is a somewhat rigid design and therefore may have limitations to its ability to modularize. This is because the base building block of a mechanized unit is the fusion of an armored vehicle and an infantry section.

While the second mechanized battalion enhances the capability of a hardened Army, the limit of modularity may impede the ability to orchestrate unique tailored forces, especially interagency elements or non-traditional battalion-group assets. As highlighted by the CDF in *'Force 2020',* to develop the seamless force, means that all services and agencies (regardless of supporting or supported relationships) must be integrated operationally with each other, including externally and cross functionally.[146] This implies that force structure must also embrace the ability to achieve synergy associated with a national effects-based approach demanded by Government.[147]

In an age of protean insecurity, it will be rare to employ an infantry battalion on what was previously termed 'conventional operations'. In the complex environment, operations will take place under 'special conditions'. The infantry battalion needs the ability to be utterly flexible in carrying out missions. This demands that the standard modus operandi of an infantry battalion must be able to flex and change according to the environment, conditions and required tasks[148].

This is where the rigidity of the mechanized structure may be exposed as a limitation. A mechanized battalion may be modular in structure, however does it have the ability to reconfigure

---

[145] Huba Wass de Czege, and Richard Hart Sinnreich. *Conceptual Foundations of a Transformed US.* [Online] ; available from The Institute For Land Warfare, Association Of The United States Army, http://www.ausa.org/PDFdocs/lwp40.pdf

[146] Australian Department of Defence. *Future Warfighting Concept.* 2003: 17.

[147] Ibid,. 32. Force design must be able to cater for the capability to conduct war fighting and other operations, such as peace operations or law-enforcement tasks where the application of violence is not a primary need. Force constructs may include small military components supporting other agencies.

and adapt to unique or special conditions? The ability for a mechanized structure to incorporate tailored designs with non-traditional battalion assets or interagency teams may be questionable. This raises an important capability question for the Australian Army. Should the hardening concept establish a rigid mechanized structure or adopt an approach that allows Army the capability to mount infantry forces where requirements dictate? This question will be addressed in the flowing chapter.[149]

---

[148] Alan Ryan *Putting Your Young Men in the Mud.* Study Paper no. 124, Land Warfare Studies Centre, Duntroon, Canberra, Australia, November 2003: 9

[149] For the purpose of this paper, the definition of a mechanized unit is an organization that possesses organic armored infantry fighting vehicles. The basic Infantry sections or Squad consists of the vehicle, the section commander, driver, and seven soldiers. A mounted capability is based on an armored unit with the capacity to carry soldiers, protect and support soldiers while operating in an environment. The mounted ability is considered a temporary relationship, where armored assets support designated elements for set tasks, phases or duration of operations. The armored vehicle commander and driver are armor corps soldiers which belong to a parent armored unit.

CHAPTER FIVE

AN ALTERNATIVE APPROACH FOR GOVERNMENT: "THE HARDENED MODULAR FORCE"

This chapter presents an alternative modular force structure design that may offer advantages for the desired hardened force over the current proposal. If one is serious about the tenets of flexibility and versatility, defined in Appendix A, then one should not overlook the complete modular construct design detailed below in figure 4.

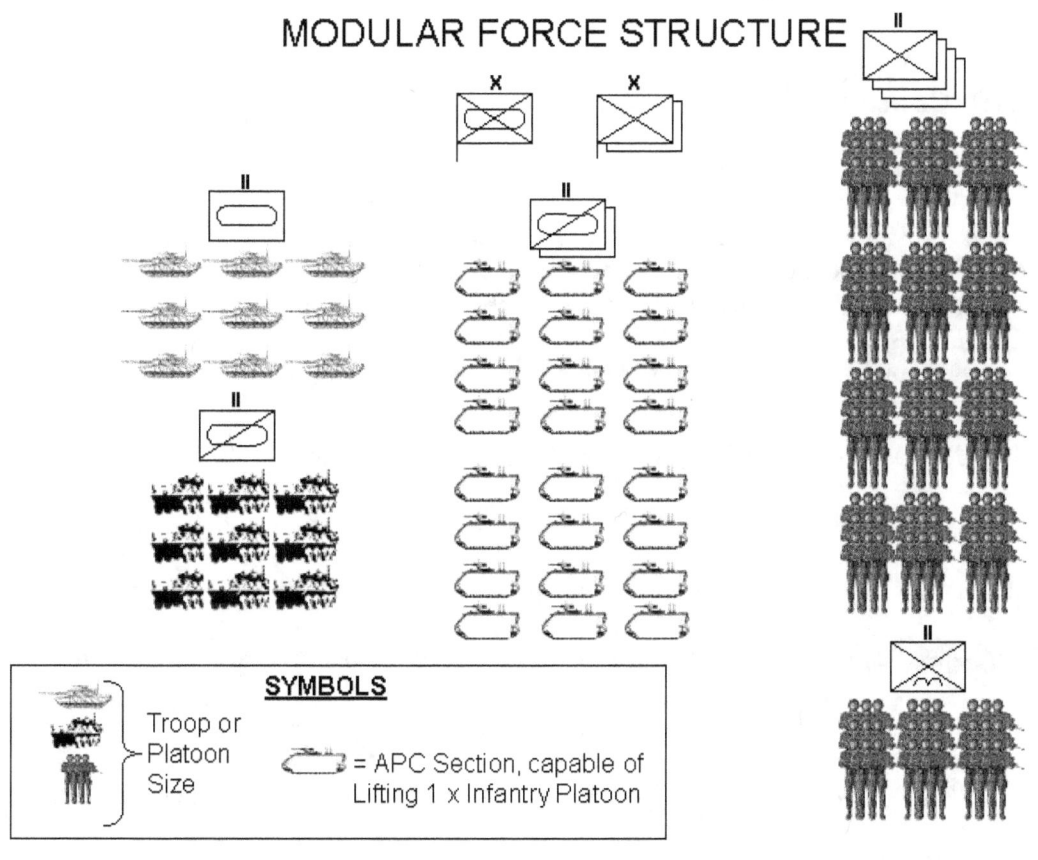

Figure 4 - Alternative Hardened Modular Force Structure Design

The alternative hardened modular force proposal emphasizes capability over functionality, challenging the dialectic between the established functional structure of two mechanized battalion capabilities versus the capability to, when required, mount two infantry battalions in armor protected vehicles or alternative mission designed configurations.

If Government is serious about the ability to have options, and Army is committed to be able to build tailor designed forces for deployment, then this proposal may outweigh the advantages offered by a mechanized unit structure. The USMC MAGTF model serves as a useful example to discuss modular designs.[150] To highlight why this alternative design should be considered, this chapter will discuss aspects of the MAGTF construct, future Australian task force constructs, resource limitations of the Australian Army, the factors of operational art, training liability comparisons between modular and mechanized designs, and highlight other US modular based concepts.

US MAGTF Concept

> The Marine Corps will enhance its strategic agility, operational reach, and tactical flexibility to enable joint, allied, and coalition operations and interagency coordination. These capabilities will provide the geographic combatant commanders with scalable, interoperable, combined-arms Marine Air-Ground Task Forces (MAGTFs) to shape the international environment, respond quickly to the complex spectrum of crises and conflicts, and gain access or prosecute forcible entry operations.[151]

The US Marine Corps typically will force organize for operations as scalable, tailorable, combined arms teams called MAGTFs. The MAGTF is a balanced purpose built, air-ground combined arms task organization of Marine Corps forces under a single commander, structured to accomplish a specific mission. The US Marine Corps use this modular construct to design forces for all missions across the spectrum of operations. The MAGTF is purpose built to fight while having the ability to prevent conflicts and control crises. They will vary in size and capability according to the assigned mission, threat, and environment.[152]

---

[150] MAGTF = Marine Air Ground Task Force. See U.S. Department of the Navy. Headquarters United States Marine Corps. *Expeditionary Maneuver Warfare,* Washington, D.C: Government Printing Office, November 2001:6

[151] U.S. Department of the Navy. Headquarters United States Marine Corps. *Marine Corps Strategy 21,* Washington, D.C: Government Printing Office, November 2000.1

[152] MCDP 1-0 "Marine Corps Operations" describes how Marine Corps forces support the joint or multinational force commander and what capabilities the Marines bring to a joint or multinational force. It illustrates how the Marine Corps' task-organized combined arms forces, flexibility, and rapid deployment

As a modular organization, the MAGTF is tailorable for assigned missions through flexible task organization. This building block approach also makes reorganization a matter of routine. Additionally the MAGTF structure can adapt to include multinational forces and/or interagency assets.[153] It is suggested that the modular concept offered by the MAGTF structure allows greater flexibility then any mechanized design.

Future Task Forces

It is important to understand the likely configurations of the future force and the challenges these create. Government states that the greatest challenge to an effects-based-approach is the degree of integration/interaction with national agencies.[154] Tailored forces will include a mixture of joint, interagency and specialized capabilities known as JIATF's.[155] Tailored forces will also include additional specialists such as linguists and humanitarian specialists.[156] Configurations will be task dependant demanding a flexible suite of capabilities. Operation Anode, the 2003 Australian-led deployment to the Solomon Islands, is an example of these requirements, where a tailored force included light infantry (capable of being mounted in APCs), ASLAV troops, a purpose designed JIATF (Department of Foreign Affairs and Trade (DFAT), and a large federal police contingent.[157]

Future task forces optimized for complex warfighting will operate in small, semi-autonomous teams. These teams incorporate the key elements of a combined arms team including

---

capabilities apply to the widening spectrum of employment of today's military forces. U.S. Department of the Navy. Headquarters United States Marine Corps. *Marine Corps Operations MCDP 1-0:* Washington, D.C: Government Printing Office, September 2001. 3-10 to 3-11.

[153] U.S. Department of the Navy. Headquarters United States Marine Corps. *Marine Corps Operations MCDP 1-0:* Washington, D.C: Government Printing Office, September 2001. 3-13.

[154] The Australian Government highlights that Effects based Operations (EBO) will dominate Australia's approach to complex warfighting. See: Australian Department of Defence. *Force 2020.* Canberra, Australia: National Capital printing, 2002: 22.

[155] JIATF = Joint Interagency task force. The JIATF is an organization created to integrate and synchronize strategic intentions by Government harnessing all elements of national power. For further explanation of JIATF and how standing JIATF structures are employed within the US Combatant Commands, See US Joint Publication 5-0.

[156] Leahy, Address to the Land Warfare Conference, 28 October 2003.

maneuver, firepower, situational awareness, command and control, and the ability to apply

remotely-generated offensive fires, logistics and mobility support to supplement their organic

capabilities. These teams will be tailored, mission-specific groupings that may be as small as one

or two armored fighting vehicles and a section of troops, a linguist, a humanitarian specialist and

two federal police, but function semi-autonomously in a linked, mutually supporting fashion. The

complete modular approach allows the ability to create scalable tailored forces of this

requirement.[158] It is questionable whether a mechanized unit can modularize to this level[159].

Alan Ryan recently released a paper examining the structure of today's Australian

infantry battalion, titled *Putting Your Young Men in the Mud*. While this paper does not present

force structure solutions, it lays out an excellent basis to debate force structure initiatives for the

21st Century Australian Army.[160] Ryan argues that historically, the infantry battalion group forms

the base building block for operational deployment constructs.[161] This will not always be the case

for future operations. Complex warfighting demands Army to provide forces, not for one big

effort against a clearly identifiable foe, but force packages capable of dealing with a range of

different, but simultaneous crises. Rigid and inflexible unit establishments, such as the

---

[157] Australia Department of Defence. *Complex Warfighting* 2003: Annex A-1.

[158] Ibid., 14.

[159] As previously highlighted the base building block of the mechanized unit is the fusion of an armored vehicle and an infantry section/squad. While both assets may be able to operate separate from each other, there is limited ability to incorporate extrinsic elements unless they are too configured in an armored vehicle.

[160] Alan Ryan *Putting Your Young Men in the Mud.* Study Paper no. 124, Land Warfare Studies Centre, Duntroon, Canberra, Australia, November 2003. This paper looks at the evolution of the Australian Army since Australian federation in 1900. It highlights the various forms of influence to the modern infantry battalion through to expectations of tomorrow's infantry structure. The paper sets the framework for further professional research and comment relating to the future force structure of the Australian Army.

[161] Ibid,. 26. Ryan states," when a battalion is deployed, the headquarters of the battalion is likely to become the command element of a battalion group and it will be provided with engineers, military police, aviation? even armour and artillery? to enable it to perform the task required of it. The multi-dimensional tasking of an infantrybased battalion group involves preparing for contingencies that far exceed the inherited shibboleth of the Pentropic era." This concept is based on historical data from deployments of Infantry Battalion groups to Somalia, East Timor and recently the Solomon Islands.

mechanized battalion of the industrial-age, may not meet the complete needs of the complex environment.[162]

The complex warfighting environment demands light infantry, supported by armored platforms as the basis for the future force. One of the principle military lessons of OEF in Afghanistan is that advanced armies continue to require 'dismount-led' combined arms forces for close combat in potentially complex terrain.[163] Historically, the Australian Army is renowned for its high quality, well-trained light-infantry based contingents supporting multinational operations. Given the current policy guidance from Government, it is unlikely that this characteristic will change.[164]

Force Structure Limitations – Mechanized Infantry

The mechanized infantry battalion structure may be limited in its ability to adapt or act as a dynamic basis for force deployment packages.[165] To understand this perspective one should ask why the current in-service mechanized battalion (5/7 RAR) deployed to East Timor (INTERFET)

---

[162] Ibid,. 9. Ryan's comments form a basis to question the very concept of a second mechanized battalion. If one considers that mechanization is a product of the industrial age and the fact that mechanization = an inherent infantry centric rigidity, then alternative non-rigid options should be examined.

[163] Stephen Biddle, Afghanistan and the Future of Warfare: Implications for Army and Defense Policy, Strategic Studies Institute, US Army War College, Carlisle, PA, November 2002:57.

[164] Alan Ryan. Australian Army Cooperation with the Land Forces of the United States, Problems of the Junior Partner. Study Paper no. 121, Land Warfare Studies Centre, Duntroon, Canberra, Australia, 2002: 11.

[165] Brendan Kirby, Chris Martin, Angela Horseman and Yi Yue, *Enhancement of a Tailorable Defence Architecture Modeling Tool*. Land Operations Division, Defence Science and Technology Organisation (DSTO), Edinburgh, Jun 2003. This report looks at the various tools that provide Land forces with assistance in designing flexible and adaptive force structures. In particular, the focus of this study is on command and control options. This report highlights that military has indicated future requirements for deployable forces will need to have an intrinsically flexible force structure. Battle grouping is an enabling concept that allows a case-by-case design of combined arms teams to achieve specific missions. Under this concept, the chain of command changes as units are re-grouped for different missions. Previously, networks followed the chain of command, now they would support the chain of command. This implies the requirement for high levels of interoperability between force elements to support a modular and flexible approach to force design.

in a predominately light configuration.[166] It is suggested that the conditions of East Timor

demanded 5/7 RAR to configure this way. This however had unfortunate second and third order

effects. One of the problems associated with mechanized infantry is the effectiveness and

efficiency of the organization when reorganized or structured for dismounted operations. The

standard configuration of the mechanized section/squad is the fusion of a nine-man section with

an armored vehicle (APC). In simplistic terms, two options essentially exist when reconfiguring a

mechanized section for dismounted operations: the vehicle and crew (two men) support a seven

man dismounted section; or all nine members of the section dismount and the APC become

unmanned.[167]

The creation of a second mechanized battalion may only achieve part of the CA's intent

for a hardened Army, because, in principle, it hardens only 40% of the regular infantry units.[168]

The modular construct has the ability to harden 100% of deployed assets, regardless of the

military or agency structure, or the dynamics of a complex environment. The modular design has

the advantage of reinforcing task force operations where required or reducing the footprint of

Australian task forces when required without disrupting the integrity of unit structures. Flexibility

is enhanced by the ability to redistribute armored assets as required (either intra or inter

theater).[169] The mechanized structure may be limited in this ability.

---

[166] 5/7th RAR deployed as part of INTERFET forces to East Timor in Oct 1999. 5/7 RAR was one of three battalion groups who operated as part of INTERFET and then remained in country as part of UN stabilization forces (UNTAET). 5/7 RAR was not required to deploy in its mechanized role (majority of vehicles remained Darwin). For more details see: Bob Breen, *Mission Accomplished – East Timor* Allen and Unwin, Australia Feb 2001

[167] 5/7th Battalion left the majority of their APC assets at home station during their deployment to INTERFET and subsequent UNTAET rotation. This resulted in significant maintenance issues for the unit upon their relocation to Australia. It is suggested that alternative resource management designs would have alleviated this dilemma. This situation complicates Army's ability to project such APC assets, if required for either training or alternative operations demands.

[168] 40% is based on the calculation of Army mechanizing two out of five infantry battalions.

[169] If one compares the deployment of an infantry battalion group, which includes an APC squadron, with the deployment of a mechanized battalion, the former structure offers flexible advantages over the mechanized structure. The battalion can insert initially without APC assets and conduct limited maneuver or deploy completed mounted for hostile threats and then once stabilized, dismount and engage

Resource Limitations – Flexibility and Balance

"Australia's material constraints present a unique problem for contending with change. Baker summed up Australia's strategic situation as "a mismatch between our ability to change and the pace of events in the world around us". Australia's perceived material and resource limitations have given latitude to a largely conservative methodology managing change. Comparatively, while Australian thinking can be broadly called 'a transformation -based strategy', it differs from the US paradigm in its recognition of the need to preserve a conservative balance in the ADF. Identifying key differences between Australian thinking and the US Transformation Paradigm are twofold. Firstly, there is the material difference in scale. Secondly, there is a different methodological emphasis."[170]

Resource constraints play an important role in deciding force design, further emphasizing the importance of a flexible structure. The Australian Army design cannot follow US Army modernization plans due to clear disparities in resources. This may mean breaking the traditional mental model of light forces and heavy forces. For example, the UK Army is looking at improving the capability of its light forces through developing what it terms "medium" forces and rebalancing heavy forces. [171] This has been based on British experiences from OIF. The UK MOD recommends that lightly equipped brigades must train and be able to integrate with heavy forces. Cross-pollination of light and heavy forces allows a multitude of force designs that provides the ability to achieve flexible depth in force design.[172] In essence, the US Stryker brigade seeks a similar capability, albeit on a different scale.[173]

---

the environment. This then frees armored assets for other needs. It is possible that a mechanized structure could tie up assets that are not necessarily required purely because they belong to that unit deployed.

[170] Christopher Flaherty "The relevance of the US Transformation Paradigm for the Australian Defence Force." *Defence and Security Analysis.* Vol 19 No 3 (September 2003): 232.

[171] Conrad C. Crane ed., *Transforming Defense.* Strategic Studies Institute, U.S. War College, Carlisle Barracks PA. 2003, 171.

U.S. Department of the Army. *The Army Strategic Planning Guidance 2006-2023.* Washington D.C: Government Printing Office, 2003, 8.

[172] United Kingdom Ministry of Defence, *Operations in Iraq.* Directorate General Corporate Communications DCCS (Pubs) London December 2003, p22. Note: The British Strategic Defence Review (SDR) envisages the development of an expeditionary-based capability, providing ready, balanced forces capable of applying decisive effect in scenarios of varying intensity, frequency and character in an uncertain and unpredictable world. See: United Kingdom Ministry of Defence, *Operations in Iraq.* Directorate General Corporate Communications DCCS (Pubs) London December 2003, p8.

[173] Looking again at aspects from the U.S. Army Strategic Planning Guidance, The US Armies ability to successfully provide the Joint Team both rapid expeditionary capabilities and the ability to conduct sustained land campaigns across tye full spectrum of conflict requires both active and reserve

The challenge for the Australian Army differs. Rebalancing must not focus purely on combat arms or supporting arms. Complex warfighting demands that any quest for balance and flexibility will need to be applied across the spectrum of all branches of Army, specialists and interagency.

The alternative modular design allows operational artists the capability to force package innovative groupings using limited and sometimes scarce resources. "In the Australian context, the adaptation of innovation is contained on the one hand by limited resources, and on the other by the need to minimize gaps in capability".[174] Innovative organizations are also unlikely to be purely infantry or combined arms based. They will instead consist of combinations of combined arms, support, and service support with elements of DFAT, federal police, and special envoys. A new paradigm exits in the complex domain where protected ground mobility is not infantry centric.[175] Army capabilities must therefore be able to offer hardening principles to the complete JIATF. The modular capability based design is a dynamic structure that can achieve such desire.

Defence 2020 states that flexibility and adaptability allows the ADF to meet significant challenges across the spectrum of operations. It also presents the ADF with the state-of-mind that dogma or rigid factors do not bound force structure. Resourcefulness within Army allows planners to develop smart ideas, test them, implement them, and more generally, to develop the

---

component contributions. The US will restructure the current force creating modular capabilities and flexible formations U.S. Department of the Army. *The Army Strategic Planning Guidance 2006-2023.* Washington D.C: Government Printing Office, 2003, 8.

[174] Flaherty "The relevance of the US Transformation Paradigm for the Australian Defence Force." 2003: 230.

[175] Huba Wass de Czege *"New Paradigm" Tactics: A Primer on the Transformation of Land Power* Emailed by LTC Richard Dixon [richard.dixon@us.army mil], G3 CAC HQ, US Army Fort Leavenworth, 24 Oct 2003, 82. Huba Wass de Czege highlights that the new paradigm is for robust and survivable "networked" organizations that "see first, understand first, act first, and close to finish decisively. This does not imply a monopoly on infantry platforms, but joint, interagency and multinational. As a rule, casualties within combat forces will occur most often when situational awareness and mobility are lost. The most vulnerable portions of the force as a whole are not combat forces at all, but those located in stationary facilities, without force protection platforms and in relatively more predictable locations. Using the de Czege model, if hardening is directly related to a survivable force then force protection must be holistic across any force package the Australian Army may deploy.

best options possible with limited resources.[176] The alternative modularized construct allows planners such latitude.

The ability to provide soldiers on the ground across the full spectrum of operations remains Army's indispensable contribution to national interests.[177] Limited resources, for example armored protected vehicles, impose numerous limitations on Army's ability to generate sustainable force packages.[178] Force structure options should therefore favor designs premised on the ability to tailor resources for operations over any option that fuses capability into organic structures. Arguably the later construct restricts ones ability to perform operational art.

Operational Art and Flexibility

To perform operational art, one must have the capability to build, deploy, engage, the ability to re-orientate, re-organize, re-engage and then re-deploy forces within an interagency construct to achieve strategic objectives.[179] It is questionable whether the creation of a second mechanized battalion adds value to the operational flexibility demanded of the Australian Army or may restrict such flexibility. To answer this question, one should consider the multitude of designs available to the operational artist from the modular construct in comparison to the mechanized structure.

Dr Ryan from the Land Warfare Studies Centre states that: "too often, the architects of strategic policy seem to regard force structure as written in stone, inviolable and sacrosanct. But

---

[176] Australian Department of Defence. *Force 2020.* Canberra, Australia: National Capital printing, 2002: 6.

[177] Lieutenant General Peter Leahy, AO, Address to the Australian Command and General Staff College, Canberra, 25 March 2003, [On-line]; available from www.defence.gov.au/army

[178] Historically, the Australian Army has been a light force due to mobilization constraints (easier to raise train and sustain light infantry), limited procurement of large quantities of principle military items has also been unfeasible due to budgetary constraints and Australia's size. In comparison to service such as the Navy, the Australian Army is people centric versus platform centric.

[179] "Operational Art is at the center of Australian Army thinking on the conduct of war. Operational art is the skilful employment of military forces to attain strategic goals through the design, organization, sequencing and direction of campaigns and major operations. It translates strategy into operational and ultimately tactical action." Australian Department of Defence. *Future Warfighting*

such inflexibility is the antithesis of good strategy which results from measuring risk against

probability and cost to determine capability."[180] Taking this concept one step further, the

capability to mount two infantry battalions or construct mounted combined task forces purpose

built for operations may outweigh the flexibility of a rigid mechanized formation. As suggested

by Dupont, the Army needs to be a far more agile, flexible, mobile, multi-skilled and innovative

organization than in the past.[181] Mechanized forces could be interpreted, as an organization of the

past, while modular constructs are a path for the future.

Novel force constructs do not imply any reduction in the lethality, ability or application

of infantry in complex environments. The modular hardened structure allows the operational

artist to tailor forces for a broad spectrum of operations. Hardening is not about making the

infantryman's load heavier. As highlighted by Ryan: "Hardening the Army' is in large part about

lightening the infantryman's load and making Australian infantry as effective, efficient and lethal

as it can be."[182] Army should pursue design models, where combinations of vertical and ground

maneuver deliver them to the fight in the peak of condition. A mechanized structure may prohibit

these desires[183]

The modular construct allows the operational artist flexibility in the manner units are

rotated and the sustainment of operational deployments. For example, a deployment that requires

a tank squadron, reconnaissance squadron, and three mounted infantry companies, could sustain

three 6 month rotations, before units where tasked to recycle. US experiences in Iraq suggest that

this ability may be of significant importance.[184]

Concept. Canberra, Australia: National Capital printing, 2003: 30. Operational art is also described in the *Australian Defence Doctrine Publication* series, especially *ADDP 3 – Operations.*

[180] Alan Dupont. "Transformation or Stagnation? Rethinking Australia's Defence." *Australian Journal of International Affairs.* Vol. 57 (April 2003): 70.

[181] Ibid,. 71.

[182] Ryan *Putting Your Young Men in the Mud.* 2003: 3-4.

[183] Ibid.,

[184] East Timor is a good example to highlight this issue.

Liability Comparisons Between Modular and Mechanized Designs

A contrast in training and maintaining liabilities exists between the current hardened structure and the alternative modular design. In a mechanized infantry battalion, armored vehicle skills are trained and maintained by the infantry corps or the supporting arm/service with a habitual relationship to a mechanized unit. In the modular construct, armored vehicle skills become solely an armored corps function. In the mechanized design, the service and maintenance of armored assets is born by the organic unit, whereas in the modular design this is centralized again under armored unit structures. The mechanized structure decentralizes armored skills and maintenance, while the modular structure centralizes such aspects. There are advantages to both concepts. [185]

The mechanized structure of infantry and organic armored vehicles is likely to achieve an enhanced infantry-armored capability over an ad-hoc created organization. This development is logical, particularly given that a mechanized battalion owns its organic armored vehicles, allowing an increased awareness and greater opportunity for training. The modular construct is disadvantaged, as modular units must request training support to achieve a similar standard of expertise.

The converse exists when considering maintenance liabilities. The mechanized unit is responsible for repair and maintenance of its organic armored fleet, which in many instances detracts from a unit's ability to concentrate on core business. In the modular design, non-armored units are not responsible for repair or maintenance. This subsequently allows these units to concentrate on their respective core skills without associated distractions.

---

[185] The perspective of centralized versus decentralized armor capability was generated through discussion with LTCOL Rob Manton, the current Australian exchange officer at US CGSC. LTCOL Manton previously commanded the Artillery Regiment in Darwin, responsible for providing offensive support (OS) to the current heavy Australian Brigade. As CO of this unit, he was responsible for providing mounted OS capability to the current mechanized Battalion 5/7 RAR. The decentralized aspects of armored vehicle management created an unnecessary administrative burden on his unit and in many ways deprived his ability to focus on the core business of OS. Interview LTCOL Manton 16 Feb 2004.

It is suggested that the centralized attributes employed by the modular design provide an important economic advantage over the mechanized structure. The modular design allows units an increased freedom to concentrate on skill sets correlated to their respective role in complex warfare. The modular deign also allows enhanced dismounted capability over the mechanized structure. When a mechanized section/squad dismounts from their vehicle, they operate as a seven-man team. A modular model mounts and dismounts nine-man sections. In essence, the modular design offers the infantry commander the ability to dismount and operate two additional riflemen per section/squad. This is an important advantage.[186]

Other Modular Designs

Murray and O'Leary observe that, "planners should think about transformation in terms of how best to combine new concepts in war with new technologies in order to extend capabilities rather than radically transform the armed forces as a whole."[187] Two US concepts applicable to the proposed hardened Australian modular design are offered in Grange and associates concept of Air-Mech strike and McNaughter's rapid light-medium strike force.

In Grange and associates model, light forces are multipurpose forces, capable of airborne or air-assault forced entry, similar to the Australian MOLE concept.[188] Once committed, Grange sees army helicopters as the primary provider of light unit mobility on the battlefield. The Air-

---

[186] The standard Australian Army Infantry section is based on a nine men. In a mechanized unit, the nine man section is reduced to seven dismounts because the driver and crew commander remain with their respective vehicle. The Modular construct has independent vehicle crew who are not integral to the basic section structure.

[187] Murray, W. O'Leary, T 'Military Transformation and Legacy Forces', *Joint Force Quarterly*, No. 30, (Spring 2002) Institute for National Strategic Studies: National Defense University, 27.

[188] Key capabilities required for the Australian Army to conduct MOLE include: speed, mobility in complex terrain and survivability by armored protection with integral fire support. See Brian H. Cooper "Army and MOLE" *Asia-Pacific Defence Reporter*, September 2003: 15.

Mech-Strike concept improves light unit tactical mobility by augmenting light armored track or wheeled vehicles to light infantry units when required.[189]

McNaughter's approach is that the US Army must offer new and different combinations of combat power and high responsiveness. He sees the new medium-weight stryker brigades as the basis for a rapid light-medium strike force, tailor built without any resemblance to the full brigade. A task force design that integrates Special Operations Forces, Rangers, combat aviation, and mounted infantry in light, wheeled vehicles that can rapidly deploy, offering considerable firepower and armored mobility. McNaughter highlights the need to emphasize modular capabilities over any traditional construct, where small elements of only the most essential capabilities for a given mission are quickly task-organized and deployed.[190] These attributes can equally be applied to the modular construct presented in this chapter.

Why the Modular Force

The Australian Army may achieve an enhanced hardened intent by adopting a capability based modular design over a mechanized structure. Using the basis of the MAGTF concept, the Australian Army may be able to establish a design basis that allows a multitude of enhanced task force options for Government that exceed those offered by mechanized structures. This modular design may also be better placed to generate an air maneuver battle group that includes ARH, utility RW (rotary wing), FW (fixed wing), light dismounted forces, cavalry, mounted infantry, tanks, offensive support, interagency support (JIATF) or humanitarian support than any traditional structure.[191]

---

[189] David Grange, Huba Wass de Czege, Liebert, Chuuch Jarnot, Al Huber and Mike Sparks *Air-Mech Strike: Asymmetrical Maneuver Warfare for the 21st Century.* Turner Publishing Company, KY, 2002: 16-21

[190] McNaugher, Thomas L. Chapter 13, *Refining Army Transformation, to The U.S. Army and the New National Security Strategy* by Davis Lynn E., and Shapiro Jeremy, eds. (Santa Monica, CA: RAND, 2003), 298.

[191] Brian H. Cooper "The New Cavalry" *Asia-Pacific Defence Reporter*, November 2003: 30.

Historically, since the end of WWII and the advent of weapons of mass destruction, the majority of conflicts have been operations other than war, where fighting while negotiating has become the standard strategy"[192] This strategy demands dismounted led operations, where the modus operandi is to engage the populace with a tailored force that is designed to achieve national interests. If Army should transition to a more flexible, strategy-based force then the modular design may outweigh constructs offered by the mechanized model. [193]

---

[192] J Sanderson,. "Force Structuring for Uncertainty." *Australian Defence Force Journal* .No 143 (Jul/Aug 2000): 53.
　　[193] Richard G. Wilson *Australia's Defence Review 2000: A step in the Right Direction.* U.S. Army War College Strategy Research Project, U.S. War College, Carlisle Barracks PA. 2001: 14.

CHAPTER SIX

CONCLUSION AND RECOMMENDATIONS

"Deploying force beyond Australia's immediate neighborhood is perfectly consistent with the defence of Australia's vital interests and should not be construed as fighting someone else's war or developing a costly, expeditionary force. In an interconnected world the ADF cannot be designed to defend a fictional moat by pulling up the drawbridge of fortress Australia when a threat suddenly materializes, for modern war is waged on a global battlefield and our enemies may already be within the castle keep." Allan Dupont 2003[194]

The CA's hardening initiative is a positive move forward to restructure the Australian Army to operate in the future threat-ambiguous strategic environment of warfare. This environment demands a force structure that is flexible, balanced and adaptive, with enhanced force protection, firepower, and agility. For some, the very nature of future warfare or the application of the Australian military instrument of power is misunderstood. For others, budgetary constraints inhibit the ability of Army to seek robust force designs. The CA's stated intent for the hardened Army is the development of a light armored force. [195] Such endeavors must occur within realistic confines and require communication with the wider Army.

Many elements within Defence struggle with the dialectic regarding what should drive the future structure of the Australian Army. Contrasting perceptions exist between the capability to deploy land forces to fight in foreign conflict, the focus on counter-terrorist capabilities, and the traditional DOA doctrine. The CA's hardening concept correctly addresses this dilemma, directing that it would be wrong for Australia to focus on any one of such option.[196] Australia can no longer classify national interests from a perspective coterminous with territory. Force structure must be postured to cater for all three requirements.

To harden the Australian Army, requires an ability to rethink strategic imperatives and adjust from traditional mindsets. While many recent lessons are available from experiences in

---

[194] Dupont. "Transformation or Stagnation? Rethinking Australia's Defence." 2003: 70.
[195] See Leahy, Address to the United Service Institution of the Australian Capital Territory, Australia, 11 June 2003.

East Timor, the Solomon Islands, Afghanistan and Iraq, such experiences have not biased proposed capability or force structure. This paper has examined the current FLW solution designed to achieve the CA's hardened concept. While this proposal is sound in principle, there are alternative options that may suit the CA's intent with greater degree. This paper presents an alternative modular construct (derived from the US Marine Corps MAGTF concept) that may be advantageous.

Why Army Must Change

Strategic guidance demanding a modernized Australian Army is published in two key documents: *Australia's National Security: A Defence Update 2003* and the *Defence Capability Plan 2003* (DCP). These strategic policy documents indicate a paradigm shift in Australian defense policy from the traditional DOA doctrine to the dialectic between Australia's geographical and global interests. While there are contrasting opinions amongst Defence circles regarding future warfare and force structure requirements of the military, a common thread exists; the Army must change to meet new demands.[197] A popular belief within Defence circles is that the Australian Government wanted to make a far more significant contribution to Iraq (OIF) than it did in Afghanistan (OEF), however no credible and acceptable military option existed.[198]

The Hardening Proposal

The FLW hardening force structure proposal upgrades the current in-service MBT and reorganizes the ground components of the Australian Army into two mechanized infantry battalions, and 3 light infantry battalions, each standardized with three rifle companies. A

---

[196] Leahy "A Land Force for the Future: The Australian Army in the Early 21st Century." 2003: 19.

[197] See Monk, Paul. *Rethinking the Defence of Australia.* [On-line] Available from Austhink www.austhink.org/monk/dibb htm

[198] See articles: Alan Dupont. "Transformation or Stagnation? Rethinking Australia's Defence; John Essex-Clark, "Niche Forces: First thoughts from an Army Perspective; and Defence articles written by Defence Journalists: Paul Vaughn, Mark Forbes, Ian McPhedran, Mark John Thompson, and Patrick Walters.

replacement tank is key to the hardened Army concept because, from a combined arms perspective, it creates a more balanced, versatile, agile and flexible force. Historical DSTO research supports the upgrade of the MBT, highlighting that the presence of a modernized tank in complex terrain has the ability to reduce casualty ratios by a factor of ten.[199]

The creation of two mechanized battalions achieves greater balance and adaptability for the Australian Army through increased versatility, agility and orchestration.[200] This structure creates the flexibility for the development of robust, combined arms teams. This paper suggests that while this concept is sound in principle, there may be some limitations, in particular in the ability for a mechanized force to achieve desired levels of modularity. This is because the base building block of a mechanized unit is the fusion of an armored vehicle and an infantry section. This may therefore preclude the ability to orchestrate unique tailored forces, especially interagency elements or non-traditional battalion-group assets.

The alternative Modular Design

An alternative modular force structure solution may be a more suitable construct for the hardened Army. This paper suggests that the ability to tailor a modular force, commensurate with Australian national interests provides an advantage over the proposed FLW mechanized model. In essence, this is because of the inherent advantages of balance, operational flexibility and adaptability that brigading of armored mobility assets into APC regiments offers versus the mechanization of two infantry battalions.

To understand the advantages of the modular design, one should consider the translation of the CA's hardened force in capability terms. Such terms demand the design of tailored force deployment packages that can expand or contract regardless of military branch or agency

---

[199] See: Michael Evans and Alan Ryan ed. *From Breitenfeld to Baghdad Perspectives on Combined Arms Warfare*. (Duntroon, Canberra, Australia: Land Warfare Studies Centre, Working Paper no. 122), 2003:58.
[200] These terms are defined in Appendix A, Method of Evaluation.

composition. As suggested by General Schoomaker, the chief of Staff of the US Army, modularity is an important facet of future force design, because that is exactly how we are operating in Iraq today.[201] The ability to tailor a discrete package of force elements creates opportunities to ensure forces that are flexible, scalable and adaptable to meet the demands of the complex environment.

Conclusion

> What is certain about the future is that even the best efforts to predict the conditions of future war will prove erroneous. What is important, however, is to not be so far off the mark that visions of the future run counter to the very nature of war and render American forces unable to adapt to unforeseen challenges. An embrace of the uncertainty of war, balanced Joint Forces, effective joint integration, and adaptive leaders will permit the flexibility that is key to future victories.[202]

The intent of this paper has been to provide an understanding of the CA's hardening concept and contribute to the debate regarding force structure development for the Australian Army. The development of military capability requires long-term investments in people, equipment and facilities. Before making any decision regarding the future structure of the Australian Army, it would be wise to solicit feedback from all sectors of Defence. This factor will become increasingly important as Army's like Australia pursue technological and structural change. One must remain cognizant that force change cannot be turned on and off like a tap.[203] The wider Defence community must therefore pursue a holistic appreciation of all possible force structure options.

At minimum, the alternative option presented in this paper serves as a useful medium to help generate an understanding and create further debate regarding the solution for the desired

---

[201] Interview with General Schoomaker, by Joseph Galloway 16 Jan 2004 [On-line]; available form http://www.realcities.com/mld/krwashington/7729049 htm

[202] McMaster, Crack in the Foundation: Defense Transformation and the Underlying Assumption of Dominant Knowledge in Future War, 2003, 98.

[203] Thompson, *Pay your Money and Take your Pick: Defence Spending Choices for Australia.* 2003.

hardened Army. As highlighted in JV2020, the ADF needs a force structure design that is robust, dynamic and above all flexible. The alternative modular design presented in this paper is a possible solution that may help path the achievement of such desires.

Recommendations

Research conducted in this paper suggests the following recommendations:

1. The Australian Army promotes a collaborative environment to understand and develop solutions for the hardened Army.

2. The alternative modular force structure design proposed in this paper serve as a basis for further debate.

3. DSTO conduct historical research to objectively compare mechanized combined arms teams with mounted combined arms teams.

4. Should the modular concept prove favorable for Army, action occurs to adjust Project LAND 106 to cater for an APC Regimental structure. [204]

---

[204] LAND 106 involves the modification of 350 M113A1 vehicles to higher standards in firepower, protection, mobility and habitually.

APPENDIX A - SELECTED METHOD OF EVALUATION

If the purpose of the Australian Army is to serve Australian national interests, then this fact should act as the catalyst for any force design evaluation. As suggested by Greg de Somer in his Land Warfare Studies Paper on future Army concepts, if Army is to best serve Australian national interests then this must be reflected in force structure. While the Army should opt for flexible forces, task-organized force capable of multiple missions, it should not go to extremes. It may be neither possible, nor desirable, to design the ultimate 'Swiss Army Knife' force structure.[205] If the need exists for a flexible, versatile, modular and more agile force to serve a whole-of-government approach to Australian national interests, and deal with a broad range of non-traditional threats, then force structure changes must occur to reflect this.[206]

In this monograph, three key source documents have been selected as base references to derive criteria for the paper's method of evaluation. Theses are: the Australian Army, Land Warfare Doctrine 1 (LWD 1): *The Fundamentals of Land Warfare,* Future Land Warfare Branch (Australian Army) *Complex Warfighting* (Draft version 3.2); and Huba Wass de Czege and Richard Hart Sinnreich, *Conceptual Foundations of a Transformed US Army.*

Using de Somers guidance, the definitions from the above three key research references and a synthesis of research material for this paper; the terms: 'balance and adaptability'; and 'flexibility and modularity' will be employed as the two broad categories to evaluate research in this paper.[207] In some ways these terms inter-relate. To assist, explanations of each term has been provided.

---

[205] Greg de Somer, The Implications of the United States Army's Army-After-Next: Concepts for the Australian Army. Land Warfare Studies Centre, Duntroon, Canberra, Australia, 1999: 29.

[206] Greg de Somer, The Implications of the United States Army's Army-After-Next: Concepts for the Australian Army. Land Warfare Studies Centre, Duntroon, Canberra, Australia, 1999: 15.

[207] Synthesis of research documents which highlight the importance of the terms 'balanced and adaptive'; flexible; and modular include: Australian Department of Defence, *Defence 2000.* Canberra, Australia: Australian Government Publishing Service, 2000; *Australia's National Security: A Defence Update 2003,* Canberra, Australia: Australian Government Publishing Service, 2003; Future Land Warfare Branch, Oct 2003; Alan Ryan *Putting Your Young Men in the Mud.* Study Paper no. 124, Land Warfare

Balance and Adaptability

FLW Paper *Complex Warfighting* states that 'balance and adaptability' as the key capability factors which should drive force structure of the Australian Army. Three force multipliers are required to design a balanced and adaptive force: Versatility Agility and Orchestration. These terms are defined below.

"Versatility is the ability to execute a broader range of tasks to a higher standard. This maximizes land forces' utility across the full conflict spectrum, and allows us to adapt quickly to change or to unexpected operational circumstances. Versatility is a key element of balance.

Agility is the ability to transition between tasks quickly, smoothly, with greater stealth and better protection. This is essential in Complex Warfighting with its requirement to perform multiple tasks at the same time, in the same place, with the same forces. It also allows the force to generate a higher tempo, a critical advantage in complex environments.

Orchestration is the ability to synchronize and coordinate effects to achieve discriminating application of force. Orchestration occurs within Army through battle grouping into combined arms teams. It also occurs within the ADF and with other government agencies through JIATFs. Orchestration with coalition partners occurs through Combined Joint Task Forces." [208]

Studies Centre, Duntroon, Canberra, Australia, November 2003; S.D. Evans, "The Defence of Australia and its' Interests." *Australian Defence Force Journal.* No 143 (Jul/Aug 2000): 31; Greg de Somer, The Implications of the United States Army's Army-After-Next: Concepts for the Australian Army. Land Warfare Studies Centre, Duntroon, Canberra, Australia, 1999; Peter Leahy "A Land Force for the Future: The Australian Army in the Early 21st Century." *Australian Army Journal.* Vol 1. (June 2003); Lieutenant General Peter Leahy, AO, Address to the United Service Institution of the Australian Capital Territory, Australia, 11 June 2003, [On-line] www.defence.gov.au/army [Accesed] 7 November 2003; and Christopher Flaherty "The relevance of the US Transformation Paradigm for the Australian Defence Force." *Defence and Security Analysis.* Vol 19 No 3 (September 2003): 240.

[208] Definitions have been extracted directly from the FLW DRAFT publication: Australian Department of Defence. *Complex Warfighting* (Draft version 3.2). Canberra, Australia: Future Land Warfare Branch, Oct 2003:17.

Flexibility and Modularity

As defined in LWD 1, **flexibility** is where the "Army possesses a balanced range of capabilities that provide options to satisfy critical strategic objectives (not based on a single means or technology and responsive to changes in the strategic environment)."[209] **Modularity** allows Army the ability to achieve **flexibility** in complex environments. **Modular forces** are the generation and structure of semi-autonomous teams working to broad central direction. By nature they are **flexible**, so that the same organization can be configured in numerous different ways.[210]

FLW, highlight that Army can best achieve this force design through adopting the modular model currently employed by Special Forces organizations worldwide.[211] This model is not limited to traditional combined arms elements. It must also include the ability to incorporate interagency elements known as Combined Joint Interagency Task Forces (JIATFs).[212] The ability to be able to **tailor** forces remains integral to any **modular** concept. This approach must balance between the dialectic of stability and agility. Designed properly, for the complex environment, **tailoring** assures the operational **agility** to conduct high-tempo operations and allowing smooth force expansion and contraction, as conditions require.[213]

---

[209] Australian Army. Land Warfare Doctrine 1 (LWD 1): *The Fundamentals of Land Warfare.* Sydney, Australia: Combined Arms Training and Development Centre, 1999:90

[210] Australia Department of Defence. *Complex Warfighting* (Draft version 3.2). Canberra, Australia: Future Land Warfare Branch, Oct 2003:14.

[211] Australia Department of Defence. *Complex Warfighting* (Draft version 3.2). Canberra, Australia: Future Land Warfare Branch, Oct 2003:14. This document states: "in order to generate numerous small semi-autonomous teams working to broad central direction but incorporating all elements of the combined arms team, unit organizations tend to be modular and flexible".

[212] Australia Department of Defence. *Complex Warfighting* (Draft version 3.2). Canberra, Australia: Future Land Warfare Branch, Oct 2003:13

[213] Huba Wass de Czege, and Richard Hart Sinnreich. [Online], The Institute For Land Warfare, Association Of The United States Army, http://www.ausa.org/PDFdocs/lwp40.pdf Accessed [22 August 2003]: 20. The author has highlighted key terms in bold to reflect the inter-relationship between the terms flexible and modular.

Method of Evaluation Notes

Background to the selected methodology criteria is provided in the following notes. In general, these have been directly extracted from the three key source documents LWD 1: *The Fundamentals of Land Warfare*, FLW *Complex Warfighting* (Draft version 3.2); and Huba Wass de Czege and Richard Hart Sinnreich, *Conceptual Foundations of a Transformed US Army* are detailed below. Aspects from other references and research material used to develop the selected method of evaluation are also detailed.

LWD - The fundamentals of Land Warfare.

LWD 1, *The Fundamentals of Land Warfare*, details six capabilities expected of the Australian Army. Theses capabilities are stated as being measures of effectiveness to determine suitability to meet government requirements.

Relevance - the Army continues to provide land forces that will contribute to defense strategy. **Credibility** - the Army provides the capability to conduct the tasks allocated by government. **Scalability** - the Army can expand and contract in a controlled fashion to meet changing security requirements. **Sustainability** - with support from other sources, the Army can maintain specified levels of commitment for the required period. **Flexibility** - the Army possesses a balanced range of capabilities that provide options to satisfy critical strategic objectives (not based on a single means or technology and responsive to changes in the strategic environment). **Efficiency** - the above measures are met using the minimum resources necessary.[214]

Future Land Warfare Complex Warfighting – Balance and Adaptability

The Future Land Warfare Paper *Complex Warfighting* specifies balance and adaptability as being the key capability factors which should drive force structure of the Australian Army.

---

[214] Australian Army. Land Warfare Doctrine 1 (LWD 1): *The Fundamentals of Land Warfare.* Sydney, Australia: Combined Arms Training and Development Centre, 1999:90

These two facets allow the force to generate a wider range of capabilities and transition between them more readily. "This balanced force can then react to a wide range of circumstances in an agile manner, removing the need to predict the future strategic environment, which Defence has historically been unable to do and which is increasingly difficult because of increasing complexity." FLW state that 'three force multipliers' are required to implement a balanced and adaptive force: Versatility Agility and Orchestration (defined above). In addition, the FLW paper highlights the need for modularity and interagency. These terms are defined below.[215]

Modularity and Interagency

"In order to generate numerous small semi-autonomous teams working to broad central direction but incorporating all elements of the combined arms team, unit organizations tend to be modular and flexible, so that the same organization can be configured in numerous different ways. Individual soldiers achieve cohesion, motivation and support through belonging to a small team that lives and trains together, generating a close-knit 'family unit'. This team may operate with a variety of other small teams to form battle groups in a variety of configurations. Close habitual training relationships, and practice in regrouping, allow units to become proficient at 'morphing' – re-grouping subordinate elements down to low levels (potentially as low as intra-platoon or intra-section regrouping) without loss of cohesion or control. This system resembles that currently adopted by Special Forces organizations worldwide, but forces optimized for Complex Warfighting tend to adopt a similar system."[216]

---

[215] Definitions have been extracted directly from the FLW DRAFT publication: Australian Department of Defence. *Complex Warfighting* (Draft version 3.2). Canberra, Australia: Future Land Warfare Branch, Oct 2003:17.

[216] Australia Department of Defence. *Complex Warfighting* (Draft version 3.2). Canberra, Australia: Future Land Warfare Branch, Oct 2003:14.

Combined Joint Interagency Task Forces.

"Complex Warfighting operations are conducted by Combined Joint Interagency Task Forces (JIATFs). These task forces incorporate all elements of national power in an integrated framework, tailored to the requirements of a specific mission."[217]

Integrated Campaigns.

"In Complex Warfighting, JIATFs execute integrated campaigns specifically tailored to the operational environment. Such integrated campaigns inter-lock military actions with a national effects-based approach (NEBA) in order to control the perceptions and behaviors of specific population groups. In this sense, an adversary group (including a regular military opponent) would form one of several populations simultaneously or concurrently targeted with military and non-military effects seeking to generate a desired outcome."[218]

US Conceptual Foundations – Future design characteristics.

This document, principally authored by Huba Wass de Czege[219], details five key design characteristics suggested for the US Army force structure design, if it is to contribute effectively to multidimensional operations at any point on the spectrum of conflict. These design characteristics are Modularity, Agility, Interoperability, Robustness and Adaptability. Definitions by Huba Wass de Czege are below.[220]

---

[217] Australia Department of Defence. *Complex Warfighting* (Draft version 3.2). Canberra, Australia: Future Land Warfare Branch, Oct 2003:13.

[218] Ibid.

[219] Brigadier General Huba Wass de Czege retired from US Army active duty in December 1993 as the Assistant Division Commander (Maneuver) of the 1st Infantry Division. He was one of the principal developers of the US Army's AirLand Battle concept and the founder and first director of the US Army School of Advanced Military Studies, (SAMS) Fort Leavenworth, Kansas. He has served as a consultant for the U.S. Army Training and Doctrine Command advanced warfighting experiments over the last seven years. He also serves as an advisor on future joint operating concepts for the Joint Staff and Joint Forces Command.

[220] Definitions and discussions of the five design principles have been extracted directly from the publication: Huba Wass de Czege, and Richard Hart Sinnreich. [Online], The Institute For Land Warfare,

Modularity

Future Army formations must reconcile operational versatility with organizational stability. Because the nature, scale and ultimate duration of ground force commitments cannot be prejudged, Army formations must be adaptable to a broad range of operational tasks without major reconfiguration, but also without forfeiting the cohesion essential to effective combat performance. That cohesion is most essential at the tactical level of engagement, where both soldiers and units are under the greatest stress, and where rapid combined-arms synchronization is most vital. Accordingly, the Army will require stable combined-arms formations at the smallest level likely to be committed independently to an operationally significant task anywhere along the spectrum of conflict.

After the tactical unit of action, paradoxically, the next most important requirement for organizational stability is at the operational level of employment. Here the challenge is less one of situational pressure than of the sheer complexity of operational command, control and sustainment functions. It also is here that multi-service; multi-agency and coalition activities routinely will be coordinated. Accordingly, while the size of such organizations may vary from one contingency to the next, the more functional stability that can be designed into them, the better.

It is between these two levels, at the level of tactical employment, that the opportunities and incentives for force tailoring are greatest, and where modularity can most effectively be exploited. Designed properly, future tactical units of employment should be reconfigurable as required with modular combat and combat support units, thus assuring the operational agility to conduct high-tempo operations and allowing smooth force expansion and contraction as

---

Association Of The United States Army, http://www.ausa.org/PDFdocs/lwp40.pdf Accessed [22 August 2003]: 20.

conditions require. It also is at this level that integration of active with reserve component units is likely to be most effective.

Agility.

Regardless of the nature of the contingency, operational maneuver from strategic distances will require Army forces optimized for rapid commitment on short notice to operations of uncertain magnitude and duration in undeveloped theaters. To achieve this without loss of operational momentum, units must be able to deploy quickly, engage immediately upon arrival, and expand as required concurrent with continued employment. In turn, that implies future force designs assuring unimpaired operational coherence from the initial arrival of forces in theater through completion of the military mission. Both initial and follow-on units must be deployable in integrated force packages that furnish a continuous balance of combat, combat support, sustainment and command-and-control capabilities across the services.

Modularity will contribute to agility. But the latter also will require adjusting existing and future tactical unit designs to reduce or eliminate altogether capabilities that can be more effectively furnished from pooled assets or reach-back, or that are likely be needed only in unusual circumstances or at a later stage of operations and whose deployment therefore can be deferred. Similarly, higher-level commanders must be able rapidly to shift combat support and sustainment priorities, "stack" that support when necessary on one or a few subordinate units, and do both across a broad geographic area.

The ability to shift concentrations of support rapidly from one point on the battlefield to another can vastly multiply the combat power even of smaller tactical formations, enabling them to overwhelm numerically larger enemy forces. Achieving it will require a comprehensive redesign of combat support and sustainment from the corps level down to the tactical units of action.

Finally, tomorrow's Army must be significantly more capable than today's of air maneuver and sustainment without penalty to ground tactical mobility, lethality and survivability. And it must be able to perform those functions on an operationally significant scale. That implies development of lighter, less consumption-limited combat and support platforms and the aircraft to move them, together with a sustainment system freed from reliance on early establishment of ground lines of communication. And it implies an investment in those capabilities sufficient to produce not just tactical, but rather operational results.

Interoperability.

Multidimensional operations inherently are joint and usually will be combined. Army formations therefore must be designed from the outset for routine subordination to a joint and/or combined task force, and for smooth integration with U.S. and allied air, maritime, amphibious, space and special operating forces. They likewise must be able routinely to support and be supported by non-defense agencies in areas ranging from information operations to civil security and humanitarian services. As a practical matter, it is infeasible to integrate those capabilities at every Army echelon without producing overlarge and unwieldy tactical formations. Indeed, that reality is one of many reasons echelonment remains essential.

At the operational level, at which joint and combined interdependence must be routine, both command-and-control and sustainment should be designed from the outset for support of and by sister service, allied and interagency organizations. At the tactical level, where interoperability needs are more limited, every future Army formation still must have the intrinsic capability to share information with joint, sister service and allied organizations, and the ability on short notice to receive, employ and support augmentation capabilities permitting closer integration. In turn, those augmentation capabilities need to be incorporated directly into the design of the force like other specialized force packages.

Robustness.

The principal risk confronting any military organization seeking to enhance its strategic and operational agility is that of insufficient robustness to cope with unanticipated battlefield demands or the loss or degradation of critical combat enablers. Such episodes are intrinsic to the nature of war and, because they invariably occur inopportunely, are difficult to accommodate unless provided for in advance.

The more uncertain the future commitment environment, therefore, the more essential it will be for the methods, organizations and equipment of future Army forces to "degrade gracefully" through sufficient built-in redundancy to absorb losses without becoming ineffective, and the ready availability of fallbacks for vital reach-back enablers such as fires, information, communications and sustainment. In large part, this is a matter of doctrine and training. But it also urges careful attention to organizational and equipment self-sufficiency. Thus, weapons optimized for non-line-of-sight engagement using remote sensors must nevertheless be able to function if those sensors or their communications links are damaged or destroyed. Platforms optimized for cooperative maneuver and engagement must be able to operate autonomously without fatal loss of effectiveness. Communications, navigation and sensor systems dependent on access to space platforms must be backed up by terrestrial alternatives. And units must have enough durability to operate autonomously for limited periods should reach-back support and sustainment functions be interrupted.

Adaptability.

By far the most important single design requirement of America's future Army forces will be the training and education of adaptable soldiers and leaders. The less predictable the demands for which they must prepare, the less we can afford to base their training and education on a rigidly consistent doctrinal template. Instead, future Army doctrine, education and training must be designed deliberately to accommodate uncertainty, and to foster a culture of institutional initiative and self-reliance that encourages soldiers and leaders to react calmly to the unexpected, avoid predictability, treat rapid changes in mission and environment as routine, and act aggressively within the framework of the force objective if and when forced to rely on their own resources.

Other Key Terms

Globalization is the spread of information and information technologies, along with greater public participation in economic and political processes. Globalization is changing the conduct of 21st century warfare.[221] Despite its apparent positive impact on the spread of democracy and free-market economies, globalization is likely to produce a more dangerous and unpredictable world, characterized by shifting power relationships, ad hoc security arrangements, and an ever-widening gap between the richest and poorest nations.[222]

---

[221] See Thomas Freedman, *Lexus and the Olive Tree.* New York, Anchor Books, 2000 for further discussion of Globalization and the effect on state and non-state actors.

[222] See Antulio J. Echevarria II, *Globalization and the Nature of War.* Strategic Studies Institute, U.S. War College, Carlisle Barracks PA. 2003, for further discussion on the effects of globalization on the nature of war.

APPENDIX B - CURRENT REGULAR ARMY FORCE STRUCTURE

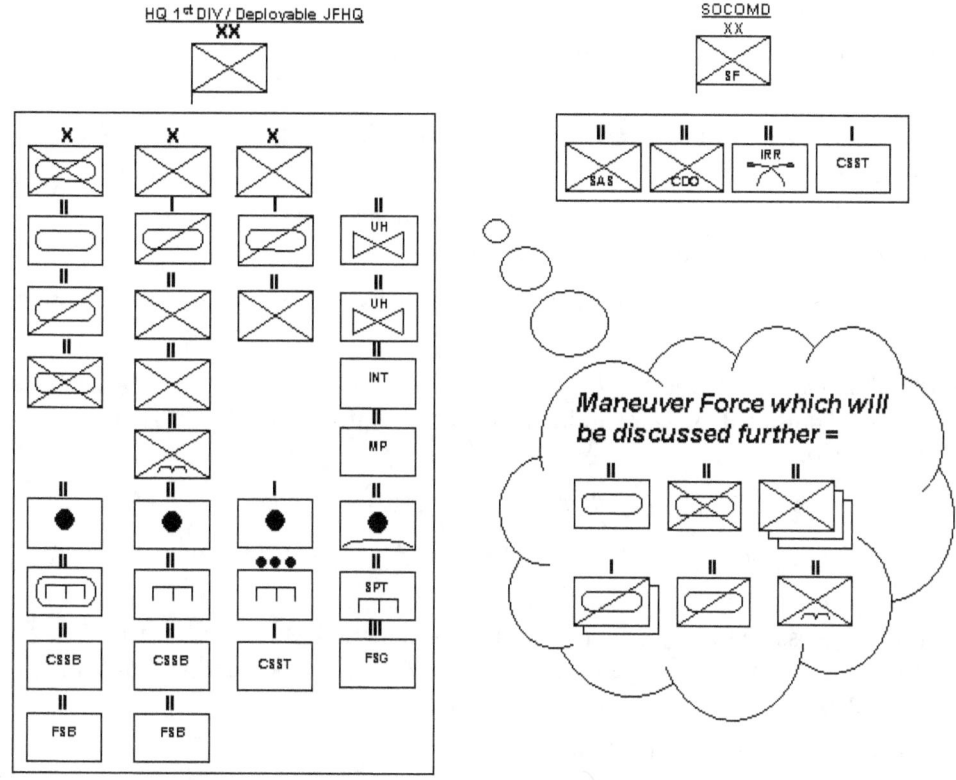

BIBLIOGRAPHY

Books

Bellamy, Christopher. *The Evolution of Modern Land Warfare: Theory and Practice.* London: Routledge, 1990.

Binnendijk, Hans, ed. *Transforming Americas Military.* Washington, DC: National Defense University Press, 2002.

Clausewitz, Carl Von. *On War.* Translated and edited by Michael Howard and Peter Paret. Princeton, NJ: Princeton University Press, 1976.

Crane, Conrad C., ed. *Transforming Defense.* Carlisle Barracks, PA: Strategic Studies Institute, U.S. War College, 2003.

Dörner, Dietrich. *The Logic of Failure: Why Things Go Wrong and What We Can Do to Make Them Right.* Translated by Rita Kimber and Robert Kimber. New York: Henry Holt and Company, 1996.

Friedman Thomas L. *The Lexus and the Olive Tree.* New York: Anchor Books, 2000.

Grey, Jeffrey. *A Military History of Australia.* Melbourne, Australia: Cambridge University Press, 1990.

Grange David, Huba Wass de Czege, Chuuch Jarnot, Al Huber and Mike Sparks *Air-Mech Strike: Asymmetrical Maneuver Warfare for the 21st Century.* Kentucky: Turner Publishing Company, 2002.

Hart B. H. Liddell. *Strategy.* New York: Signet, 1974.

_____. *Thoughts on War.* London: Faber and Faber, 1944.

Huntington, Samuel P. *The Clash of Civilizations: The Remaking of World Order.* New York: Simon and Schuster, 1997.

Knox, Macgregor, and Williamson Murray. *The Dynamics of Military Revolution: 1300–2050.* Cambridge, United Kingdom: Cambridge University Press, 2001.

Korb, Lawrence J. *Reshaping Americas Military: Four Alternatives Presented as Presidential Speeches.* New York: Council on Foreign Relations Books, Brookings Institution Press, 2002.

Luttwak, Edward N. *Strategy: The Logic of War and Peace.* Harvard: Bellknap Press, 1987.

Macquarie Concise, Dictionary. 2d ed. Sydney, Australia: The Maquarie Library Pty, Ltd. New South Wales (NSW), 1988.

McNaugher, Thomas L. Chapter 13, *Refining Army Transformation, to The U.S. Army and the New National Security Strategy* by Davis Lynn E., and Shapiro Jeremy, eds. Santa Monica, CA: RAND, 2003.

Mahan, Alfred T. *The Influence of Sea Power Upon History, 1660-1783.* New York: Hill and Wang, 1957.

Murray, Williamson, ed. *Transformation Concepts for National Security in the 21st Century.* Carlisle, PA: Strategic Studies Institute, 2002.

Naveh, Shimon. *In Pursuit of Military Excellence: The Evolution of Operational Theory.* Portland: Frank Cass, 1997.

Paret, Peter, ed. *Makers of Modern Strategy: From Machiavelli to the Nuclear Age.* Princeton: Princeton University Press, 1986.

_____. *Clausewitz and the State: The Man, His Theories, and His Times.* Princeton: Princeton University Press, 1985.

_____ . *Understanding War: Essays on Clausewitz and the History of Military Power.* Princeton: Princeton University Press, 1992.

Senge, Peter M. *The Fifth Discipline: The Art and Practice of the Learning Organization.* New York: Doubleday, 1990.

Simpkin, Richard E. *Race to the Swift: Thoughts on Twenty-First Century Warfare.* New York: Brassey's, 1986.

Sun Tzu. *The Art of War.* Translated with a historical introduction by Ralph D. Sawyer. Boulder: Westview Press, 1994.

Tone, John L. *The Fatal Knot: The Guerilla War in Navarre and the Defeat of Napoleon in Spain.* Chapel Hill, NC: The University of North Carolina Press, 1994.

Tse-Tung, Mao. *On Guerrilla Warfare.* Translated with an introduction by Samuel B. Griffith. Baltimore: Nautical and Aviation Publishing Company, 1992.

Turabian, Kate L. *A Manual for Writers of Term Papers, Theses, and Dissertations.* 6th ed. Chicago: University of Chicago Press, 1996.

Van Creveld, Martin. *On Command.* Cambridge: Harvard University Press, 1985.

_____ . *The Transformation of War.* New York: The Free Press, 1991.

Reports and Monographs

Bensahel, Nora. "Preparing for coalition Operations." *The US Army and the New National Security Strategy.* Santa Monica: RAND, 2003

Biddle, Stephen. *Afghanistan and the Future of Warfare: Implications for Army and Defense Policy.* Carlisle, PA: Strategic Studies Institute, US Army War College, 2002.

Borgu Aldo, *The Defence Capability Review 2003: A Modest and Incomplete Review.* Canberra: Australian Strategic Policy Institute, 2003.

Cheeseman, Graeme. *Army's Fundamentals of Land Warfare: A Doctrine for New Times?* Canberra: Working Paper No. 58, Australian Defence Studies Centre, April 2000.

Crane, Conrad C. *Facing the Hydra: Maintaining Strategic Balance while Pursuing a Global War Against Terrorism.* Carlisle PA: Strategic Studies Institute, US Army War College, 2002.

Deptula, BG David A. *Effects Based Operations: Change in the Nature of Warfare.* Arlington, VA: Aerospace Education Foundation, 2001.

de Somer, Greg. *The Capacity of the Australian Army to Conduct and Sustain Land Force Operations.* Duntroon, Canberra, Australia: Land Warfare Studies Centre, 1999.

_____. *The Implications of the United States Army's Army-After-Next: Concepts for the Australian Army*. Duntroon, Canberra, Australia: Land Warfare Studies Centre, 1999

Dubik, James M. *A Guide to the Study of Operational Art and Campaign Design*. Fort Leavenworth, KS: School of Advanced Military Studies, Monograph, 1991.

_____. *The Army's "Twofer": The Dual Role of the Interim Force*. Arlington VA: Land Warfare Papers No 39. The Institutue of Land Warfare, 2000.

Echevarria II, Antulio J. *Globalization and the Nature of War*. Carlisle Barracks PA: U.S. War College, Strategic Studies Institute, 2003.

Evans, Michael. *The Role of the Australian Army in a Maritime Concept of Strategy*. Duntroon, Canberra, Australia: Land Warfare Studies Centre, Working Paper no. 101, 1998.

_____. *From Deakin To Dibb: The Army and the Making of Australian Strategy in the 20th Century*. Duntroon, Canberra, Australia: Land Warfare Studies Centre, Working Paper no.113, 2001.

_____. *Australia and the Revolution in Military Affairs.* by Michael Evans. Duntroon, Canberra, Australia: Land Warfare Studies Centre, Working Paper no.115, 2001.

Evans, Michael and Alan Ryan ed. *From Breitenfeld to Baghdad Perspectives on Combined Arms Warfare*. Duntroon, Canberra, Australia: Land Warfare Studies Centre, Working Paper no.122, 2003.

Kirby Brendan, Chris Martin, Angela Horseman and Yi Yue, *Enhancement of a Tailorable Defence Architecture Modeling Tool*. Edinburgh, SA, Australia: Land Operations Division, Defence Science and Technology Organisation (DSTO), Jun 2003.

McMaster, H.R. *Crack in the Foundation: Defence Transformation and the Underlying Assumption of Dominant Knowledge in Future War*. Carlisle PA: US Army War College, Center for Strategic Leadership, November 2003.

McNaugher, Thomas L. "Redefining Army Transformation." *The US Army and the New National Security Strategy*. Santa Monica: RAND, 2003.

Metz, Steven, and James Kievit. *Strategy and the Revolution in Military Affairs: From Theory to Policy*. Carlisle PA: U.S. Army War College, Research Project, 1995.

Metz, Steven, and Raymond A. Millen. *Future War/Future Battlespace: The Strategic Role of American Landpower*. Carlisle PA: U.S. War College, Strategic Studies Institute, 2003.

Murray, Williamson, *Transformation Concepts for National Security in the 21st Century*. Strategic Studies Institute downloaded 29 Aug 03. Available from http://www.e11th-hour.org/security/transformation.concepts.html

Paret, Peter, and Daniel Moran, trans. *Carl von Clausewitz: Two Letters on Strategy*. Fort Leavenworth: Combat Studies Institute, 1984.

Ryan, Alan, *From Desert Storm to East Timor: Australia, the Asia-Pacific and the 'New Age' Coalition Operations*, Duntroon, Canberra, Australia: Land Warfare Studies Centre, Study Paper no. 302, 2000.

_____ . *Primary Responsibilities and Primary Risks: Australian Defence Force Participation in the International Force East Timor*. Duntroon, Canberra, Australia: Land Warfare Studies Centre, Study Paper no. 304, 2000.

_____ . *Australian Army Cooperation with the Land Forces of the United States, Problems of the Junior Partner.* Duntroon, Canberra, Australia: Land Warfare Studies Centre, Study Paper no. 121, 2002.

_____ . *Putting Your Young Men in the Mud.* Duntroon, Canberra, Australia: Land Warfare Studies Centre, Study Paper no. 124, November 2003.

Schneider, James J. PH.D. *The Eye of Minerva: The Origin, Nature, and Purpose of Military Theory and Doctrine.* Fort Leavenworth, KS: Command and General Staff College, 1991.

_____ . *The Theory of Operational Art.* Fort Leavenworth, KS: Command and General Staff College, 1988.

Swain, Richard M. PH.D. *Filling the Void: The Operational Art and the U.S. Army.* Fort Leavenworth, KS: Command and General Staff College, 1989.

Wilson, Richard G. *Australia's Defence Review 2000: A step in the Right Direction.* Carlisle PA: U.S. Army War College Strategy Research Project, 2001.

Articles

Akiyama, Masahiro. "Upholding Regional Security?" *Australian Defence Force Journal, no.* 143 (July-August 2000): 9-10.

Ayling, S. H. "Future Warfare Concepts: Designing the Future Defence Force." *Australian Defence Force Journal, no.* 144 (Sep/Oct 2000): 5-11.

Babbage, Ross. "New Directions for Defence: Ten Key Issues to Get Right." *Australian Defence Force Journal,* no. 143 (Jul/Aug 2000): 11-14.

Baker, J. "Australia's Defence Posture." *Australian Defence Force Journal,* no. 143 (Jul/Aug 2000): 15-18.

Barrie, C. A. "Change, People and Australia's Defence Capability for the New Century" *Australian Defence Force Journal*, no. 134 (Jan/Feb 1999): 5-15.

_____ . "The White Paper: Our Strategy." *Australian Defence Force Journal*, no. 147 (Mar/Apr 2001): 2-45.

Bell. C. "Security Regionalisation and the Future of the Australian Defence Forces." *Australian Defence Force Journal*, no.143 (Jul/Aug 2000): 21-22.

Bergin, A. "Steady As-You-Go." *Australian Defence Force Journal,* no. 147 (Mar/Apr 2001): 21-22.

Blackburn, John N., Lee Cordner and Michael A. Swan. "Not the Size of the Dog in the Fight: RMA - The ADF Application." *Australian Defence Force Journal*, No. 144 (Sep/Oct 2000): 65-69.

Boyer, Peter J. "A Different War: Is the Army Becoming Irrelevant?" *The New Yorker,* 1 July 2002, 54–67.

_____ . "The New War Machine." *The New Yorker*, 30 June 2003, 55–71.

Cheeseman, Graeme. "Choosing to Make Choices." *Australian Defence Force Journal*, no.143 (Jul/Aug 2000): 25-26.

_____ . "Revolutionising Australia's Approach to Revolutionary Times." *Australian Defence Force Journal*, no.144 (Sep/Oct 2000): 90-100.

Clark, Thea, and Terry Moon. "Interoperability for Joint and Coalition Operations." *Australian Defence Force Journal*, no.151, (Nov/Dec 2001): 23-35.

Cooper Brian H. "Army and MOLE" *Asia-Pacific Defence Reporter*, September 2003: 15.

Davies, M.J. "The Impact of the Revolution in Military Affairs on the ADF" *Australian Defence Force Journal*, no.128 (Jan/Feb 1998) 41-46.

Dibb, Paul. "The Relevance of the Knowledge Edge." *Australian Defence Force Journal*, no. 134 (Jan/Feb 1999): 37-48.

_____ . "Transforming the ADF's Force Structure for the 21st Century." *Australian Defence Force Journal*, no. 143 (Jul/Aug 2000): 27-28.

_____ . "Australia's Best Defence White Paper" *Australian Defence Force Journal*, no.147 (Mar/Apr 2001): 27-29.

Dobell, Graeme. "Educating cabinet." *Australian Defence Force Journal*, no. 143 (Jul/Aug 2000): 29-30.

Dupont, Alan. "Transformation or Stagnation? Rethinking Australia's Defence." *Australian Journal of International Affairs*, vol. 57 (April 2003): 55-76.

Evans, Michael. "Fabrizio's Choice: Organisational Change and the Revolution in Military Affairs Debate." *Australian Defence Force Journal*, no. 144 (Sep/Oct 2000): 78-89.

Evans, S.D. "The Defence of Australia and its' Interests." *Australian Defence Force Journal*. no. 143 (Jul/Aug 2000): 31-34.

Essex-Clark, John. "Niche Forces: First thoughts from an Army Perspective." *Australian Army Journal*, vol. 1 (June 2003): 11-16.

Flaherty, Christopher. "The relevance of the US Transformation Paradigm for the Australian Defence Force." *Defence and Security Analysis*, vol. 19, no. 3 (September 2003): 219-240.

Gackle, Johnathon O. "US-Australian Defence Cooperation: A Model for Twenty-first Century Security Arrangements." *Defense & Security Analysis*, vol. 18. no. 1, (2002): 39-49

Garran, Robert. "A Clever Deception." *Australian Defence Force Journal*, no. 143 (Jul/Aug 2000): 35-36.

Gentry, John A. "Doomed to Fail: America's Blind Faith in Military Technology." *Parameters*, vol. 82, no. 4 (Winter 2002-2003): 88-103.

Greer, James K., COL. "Operational Art for the Objective Force," *Military Review*, September-October 2002.

Goodyer, M. "Some Aspects of The Revolution in Military Affairs and the Impact on the ADF." *Australian Defence Force Journal*, no. 145 (Nov/Dec 2000): 15-21.

Hewish, Mark. "David V's Goliath." *International Defence Review*, 34/11 (Nov 2001): 24-36.

Hill, Richard. "Territorial Integrity and Regional Stability." *Australian Defence Force Journal*, no. 143 (Jul/Aug 2000): 37-38.

Hudson, Michael Wyndham. "Australian Government's Major Responsibilities and the Principles Underlying Defence Force Development." *Australian Defence Force Journal*, no. 143 (Jul/Aug 2000): 37-38.

Huisken, Ron. "America's New Military Roadmap for Asia and Australia." *Asia Pacific Defence Reporter,* May 2002, 40-42

Jablonsky, David. "US Military Doctrine and the Revolution in Military Affairs," Parameters, (Autumn 1994): 18-26.

Ji, You. "Revolution in Military Affairs: A New Guide for China's Military Modernisation." *Australian Defence Force Journal,* no. 144 (Sep/Oct 2000): 41-59.

Kerr Julian, "Army Focus on Close Combat and Hardening" A*sia-Pacific Defence Reporter*, November 2003: 44-45.

Kolenda, Christopher D. "Transforming How We Fight." *Naval War College Review*, vol. LVI, no. 2 (Spring 2003): 100-122.

Krepinevich, Andrew F. "The Army and Land Warfare: Transforming the Legions." *Joint Force Quarterly*, Autumn 2002, 76-82.

La Franchi, Peter. "US Pursues Common Programs with Australia. *Asia Pacific Defence Reporter,* Feb 2002, 17-18.

_____ . "Australia-US Future Armour Linkages on the Table." *Asia Pacific Defence Reporter,* May 2002, 28.

Leahy, Peter. "ANZUS: A View from the Trenches." *Joint Force Quarterly,* Autumn-Winter 1997-98, 86-90.

_____ . "A Land Force for the Future: The Australian Army in the Early 21st Century." *Australian Army Journal,* vol 1 (June 2003): 19-28.

Leonhard, Robert R. "Factors of Conflict in the Early 21st Century." *Army Magazine*, vol.53, January 2003, 31-42.

Lim, Hugh. "Impact of RMA on Command and Control: An SAF Perspective." *Australian Defence Force Journal*, no. 144 (Sep/Oct 2000): 21-26.

Lim, Robyn. "Alliances: Two-Way Streets." *Australian Defence Force Journal*, no. 143 (Jul/Aug 2000): 42-44.

Magninnis, Robert. "Keeping Our Best Army Coalition Together Relevant by Transforming Together." *Army*, (Sept 2003) 18-19.

Mak, J.N. "The RMA in South-East Asia: Security and External Defence." *Australian Defence Force Journal*, no. 144 (Sep/Oct 2000): 30-40.

McGuire, D.J. "Embracing Positive and Transformational Change in the Australian Army: A Bridge Too Far?" *Australian Defence Force Journal*, no. 152 (Jan/Feb 2002): 35-42.

Murray, W. O'Leary, T 'Military Transformation and Legacy Forces', *Joint Force Quarterly*, no. 30, (Spring 2002) Institute for National Strategic Studies: National Defense University, 27.

O'Connor, Michael. "Crafting a National Defence Policy." *Australian Defence Force Journal*, no. 143 (Jul/Aug 2000): 45-46.

O'Neill, Robert. "Australia's security needs dilemmas." *Australian Defence Force Journal*, no. 143 (Jul/Aug 2000): 47-48.

Orme, C.W. "Are We Going to Fight Again?" *Australian Defence Force Journal*, no. 141 (Mar/Apr 2000): 5-12.

Quigley, Derek. "New Directions for Australia's Defence." *Australian Defence Force Journal*, no. 143 (Jul/Aug 2000): 49-51.

Reith, Peter. "Ministers Message." *Australian Defence Force Journal*, no. 147 (Mar/Apr 2001): 3.

_____ . "The Blamey Oration." *Australian Defence Force Journal*, no. 149 (Jul/Aug 2001): 45-51.

Rolin, Xavier. "The RMA, C2 and Coalition Operations." *Australian Defence Force Journal*, no.144 (Sep/Oct 2000): 27-29.

Rumsfeld, Donald H. "Transforming the Military." *Foreign Affairs*, vol. 81, no.3 (May/June 2002): 20–32.

Sanderson, J. "Force Structuring for Uncertainty." *Australian Defence Force Journal*, no.143 (Jul/Aug 2000): 52-56.

Smith, Andrew J. "How Sharp a Sword?" *Australian Defence Force Journal*, no.132 (Sep/Oct 1998): 21-31.

Tracey, Michael P. ed. "Public Discussion Paper: Defence Review 2000." *Australian Defence Force Journal*, no.143 (Jul/Aug 2000): 2-8.

van Creveld, Martin. "The Transformation of War Revisited" *Small Wars and Insurgencies*, vol. 13, Summer 2002, 3-15.

Waranon, Werapon. "RMA in ASEAN: The Alternatives to Security." *Australian Defence Force Journal*, no.144 (Sep/Oct 2000): 60-64.

Welburn, A.C.G. "The Application of False Principles and the Misapplication of Valid Principles: A Trap for the Unwary." *Australian Defence Force Journal*, no. 124 (May/Jun 1997): 25-36.

Wing, Ian. "Australasian Defence 2048 – An Alternative Future" *Australian Defence Force Journal*, no.132 (Sep/Oct 1998): 3-11.

Young, Thomas-Durell. "Wither Future US Alliance Strategy? The ABCA Clue." *Armed Forces and Society,* 17/2 Winter, 1991, 277-297.

_____ . "Capabilities-Based Defencse Planning: The Australian Experience." *Armed Forces and Society*. Vol 21, No 3, Spring 1995, 349-369.

_____ . "Information Capabilities: An Unofficial American View." *Australian Defence Force Journal*, no.143 (Jul/Aug 2000): 57-59.

Australian Government Publications

Australian Army. Land Warfare Doctrine 1 (LWD 1), *The Fundamentals of Land Warfare.* Sydney, Australia: Combined Arms Training and Development Centre, 1999.

Australian Department of Defence. *Australia's Strategic Review.* Canberra, A.C.T: Commonwealth of Australia, 1993.

_____ . *Defending Australia: Defence White Paper 1994*, Canberra, A.C.T: Australian Government Publishing Service, 1994.

_____. *Australia's Strategic Policy*. Canberra, Australia: Australian Government Publishing Service, 1997.

_____ . *Defence 2000*. Canberra, Australia: Australian Government Publishing Service, 2000.

_____. *From Phantom to Force: Towards a More Efficient and Effective Army*. Canberra, Australia: Australian Government Publishing Service, 2000.

_____. *Force 2020*. Canberra, Australia: National Capital Printing, 2002.

_____. *Joint Warfighting Concept* (Draft version 1.3). Puckapunyal, Australia: Force Development Group, 2002.

_____. *Future Warfighting Concept*. Canberra, Australia: National Capital Printing, 2003.

_____. *Australia's National Security: A Defence Update, 2003*, Canberra, Australia: Australian Government Publishing Service, 2003.

_____. *Australian Army Journal, Volume One, Number One, Jun 2003*. Land Warfare Studies Centre, 2003.

_____. *Complex Warfighting* (Draft version 3.2). Canberra, Australia: Future Land Warfare Branch, Oct 2003.

_____. *Hardening the Army* and *Increasing Options for Government: A Harder More Capable Army*. (Unpublished). Canberra, Australia: Future Land Warfare Directorate, 2003-4.

Australian Department of Foreign Affairs and Trade. *In The National Interest*. Canberra, Australia: Government Publishing Service, 1997.

_____. *Review of Foreign Affairs, Trade and Defence Annual Reports, 2000-2001*. Canberra, Australia: Government Publishing Service, 2003.

US. Government Publications

Bush, George W. *National Security Strategy of the United States of America*. Washington: The White House, 2002.

US. Department of the Army. *Objective Force*. Washington D.C: White Paper, Government Printing Office, 1999.

_____. Field Manual (FM) 1, *The Army*. Washington, DC: June 2001.

_____. FM 3-0, *Operations*. Washington D.C: Government Printing Office, 2002.

_____. *The Army Strategic Planning Guidance, 2006-2023*. Washington D.C: Government Printing Office, 2003.

_____. *Army Transformation Roadmap*. Washington D.C: Government Printing Office, 2003.

U.S. Department of Defense. *Joint Vision 2010*. Fort Monroe: Joint Warfighting Center, 1996.

_____. *National Military Strategy of the United States*. Washington: Department of Defense, 1997.

_____. *Joint Vision 2020*, Washington D.C: Government Printing Office, 2000.

U.S. Joint Forces Command. *A Concept for Rapid Decisive Operations: RDO.* Norfolk: U.S. Joint Forces Command, White paper Version 2.0, 2001.

_____. *Joint Transformation Roadmap 03 November 2003,* Washington D.C: Government Printing Office, 2003

U.S. Marine Corps. *Marine Corps Doctrinal Publication 1, Warfighting.* Washington: Headquarters, United States Marine Corps, 1997.

U.S. Department of the Navy. Headquarters U.S. Marine Corps. *Marine Corps Strategy 21,* Washington, DC: Government Printing Office, November 2000.

_____. *Expeditionary Maneuver Warfare,* Washington, D.C: Government Printing Office, November 2001

_____. *Marine Corps Operations MCDP 1-0:* Washington, D.C: Government Printing Office, September 2001.

Internet, Newspapers and Other

Asia Pacific News, 7 November 2003. [On-line] http://asia.news.yahoo.com/031107/afp/031107080920asiapacificnews.html. Accessed on [7 Nov 2003].

Australia's 1997 Defence Policy Statement [On-Line] http://www.dfat.gov.au/arf/documents/1997defp.pdf, Accessed [07 November 2003].

Australia's Defence Capability Review Statement 2003 [Unpublished] Released by the Australian government [On-line] 07 Nov 03. http://www.defence.gov.au Accessed on [7 Nov 2003].

Barry, John. *The Bush administration's military predicament in Iraq has suddenly gotten worse.* [Online], Newsweek Web Exclusive, http://www.msnbc.com/news/962548.asp?0cv=KB20&cp1=1, Accessed [05 September 2003].

Daily Telegraph (Brisbane) November 8, 2003. [Online]: http://dailytelegraph.news.com.au/

de Czege, Huba Wass and Richard Hart Sinnreich. *Conceptual Foundations of a Transformed US.* [Online], The Institute For Land Warfare, Association Of The United States Army, http://www.ausa.org/PDFdocs/lwp40.pdf, Accessed [22 August 2003].

de Czege, Huba Wass . *"New Paradigm" Tactics: A Primer on the Transformation of Land Power.* Emailed by LTC Richard Dixon [richard.dixon@us.army.mil], G3 CAC HQ, US Army Fort Leavenworth, 24 Oct 2003, 8.

Department of the Parliamentary Library; Research Note: *Solomon Islands,* [On-Line] http://www.aph.gov.au/library/pubs/rn/2003-04/04rn04.pdf, Accessed [24 January 2004].

Dubik, James M. Landpower Essay No. 02-3, "Has Warfare Changed? Sorting Apples from Oranges," July 2002. Institute of Land Warfare database [on-line] http://www.ausa.org/PDFdocs/lpe02-3.pdf. Accessed [29 August 2003].

Evans, Michael. "Seeking the Knowledge Edge: The Revolution in Military Affairs and Its Implications for Australia." Australian Land Warfare Studies Database [On-line]. http://www.Centrejciss.llnl.gov/IT_RMA/EvansFinal.pdf. Accessed [9 September 2003].

Leahy Peter, AO, Lieutenant General, Chief of the Australian Army, Minute OCA/OUT/2003/1457, *Hardening the Army*, dated 29 August 2003.

_____ . Speeches, Available [On-Line] www.defence.gov.au/army [Accessed] 7 November 2003 through to 24 January 2004.

McLachlan, Ian. Minister for Defence, Address to the House of Representatives, 02 December 1997. [Online] http://www.defence.gov.au/minister/sr97/s971202.html Accessed [7 Nov 2003].

Monk, Paul. *Rethinking the Defence of Australia.* Database on-line from Austhink website, www.austhink.org/monk/dibb.htm, Accessed [22 August 2003].

Noonan, Michael P. *The Military Lessons of Operation Iraqi Freedom.* Foreign Policy Research Institute Database [On-line] http://www.fpri.org/enotes/20030501.military.noonan.militarylessonsiraqifreedom.html, Accessed [29 August 2003].

Rumsfeld, Donald H. "Transforming the Military." *Foreign Affairs.* May/Jun2002, Vol. 81 Issue 3, p20. Emailed by ephost@epnet.comSent: Thursday, September 04, 2003.

Scales Robert H. MG (Ret) *Statement to the House Armed Services Committee, US House of Representatives*, 21 October 2003, Washington DC: [On-line] http://www.iwar.org.uk/news-archive/iraq/lessons-learned/03-10-21-scales.html. Accessed [07 November 2003].

Sydney Morning Herald (Sydney) 7 Jan 04 [On-Line] http://www.smh.com.au/.

Thompson, Mark John *Pay your Money and Take your Pick: Defence Spending Choices for Australia.* December 2003. The Australian Strategic Policy Institute. [Online] http://www.aspi.org.au/paymoney/index.html Accessed [2 January 2004].

The Advertiser, (Brisbane) 08 November 2003. [Online] http://www.theadvertiser.news.com.au/, Accessed [08 Nov 2003].

The Age (Melbourne) 27 February – 20 November 2003. [Online] www.theage.com.au/articles, Accessed [20 Nov 2003].

The Australian and Weekend Australian (Canberra) 04 October 2003 – 5 January 2004. [Online] http://www.theaustralian.news.com.au/, Accessed [07 Nov 03 – 07 Jan 04].

U.S. Army, *White Paper, Concepts for the Objective Force*, [On-line] http://www.army.mil/features/WhitePaper/ObjectiveForceWhitePaper.pdf, Accessed [22 August 2003].

U.S. Department of Defense, *Military Transformation: A Strategic Approach.* [On-line] http://www.oft.osd.mil/library/library_files/document_297_MT_StrategyDoc1.pdf. Accessed [07 November 2003].

Wolfowitz, Paul. *Interview with The New Yorker.* Interviewer: Peter Boyer, 18 June 2002. Defenselink: [On-line] http://www.defenselink.mil/news/Jul2002/t07022002_t0618ny.html. Accessed [22 August 2003].

www.ingramcontent.com/pod-product-compliance
Lightning Source LLC
Chambersburg PA
CBHW052006280526
45793CB00005B/873